The Developing Child

Recent decades have witnessed unprecedented advances in research on human development. Each book in The Developing Child series reflects the importance of this research as a resource for enhancing children's well-being. It is the purpose of the series to make this resource available to that increasingly large number of people who are responsible for raising a new generation. We hope that these books will provide rich and useful information for parents, educators, child-care professionals, students of developmental psychology, and all others concerned with childhood.

Jerome Bruner, New School for
Social Research
Michael Cole, University of
California, San Diego
Barbara Lloyd, University of Sussex
Series Editors

The Developing Child Series

Mind and Media

The Effects of Television, Video Games, and Computers

Patricia Marks Greenfield

Harvard University Press
Cambridge, Massachusetts
1984

This book is printed on acid-free paper, and its binding materials
have been chosen for strength and durability.

Library of Congress Cataloging in Publication Data
Greenfield, Patricia Marks.
    Mind and media.
    (The Developing child)
    Bibliography: p.
    Includes index.
    1. Mass media and children.   2. Television and children.
3. Video games.   4. Child development.   I. Title   II. Series.
HQ784.M3G73 1984   305.2'3   83-18644
ISBN 0-674-57620-9 (alk. paper)
ISBN 0-674-57621-7 (pbk. : alk. paper)

To the memory of my mother,
to Matthew, and to Robert

In their individual ways,
each is a part of this book

Preface

This book represents the coming together of many strands in my intellectual and personal life. A common thread throughout my research career has been the "language-thought problem": what is the psychological relationship between language and other modes of thought? As posed in this book, the question has broadened to "What is the relationship between media of communication and the development of thought?"

In Senegal in 1963–64 I had the opportunity to observe the introduction of formal schooling and literacy into an oral culture. For the first time, I no longer took for granted the medium of print that was almost second nature in my own culture. My research on other media began in connection with the development of children's radio at KPFK, the Pacifica radio station in Los Angeles. My colleagues and I compared the effects of radio with those of television. From a theoretical point of view, print and radio provide natural foils to show what *difference* television has made as it has taken over many of the functions of these older media. This comparative perspective turned into Chapter 6.

The invitation to write this book came just as my son, Matthew, was dragging me into the computer age. I was curious to learn what microcomputers were all about and what was happening to children like Matthew who were fascinated by them. I first envisioned one chapter on children and computer technology that would be a futuristic ending to the book. But the future arrived more quickly than I anticipated; and my planned chapter mushroomed into two. As Matthew guided me through the world of video games, what had been planned as a subsection of the computer chapter grew to be a chapter in itself.

These two chapters were difficult to write because I could not come to them as any sort of an expert. In the area of video games, there were not even any experts to consult. I could only approach the subject as an anthropologist coming into a foreign culture. I wondered about the nature of the motivations and skills that children in the video/computer culture have, skills that I, as a member of a different culture, lack. I wondered why skills that were so simple and obvious for my teenage son were difficult and sometimes impossible for me. The answers I came up with are contained in Chapters 7 and 8.

Without the generous help I received from many directions, this book would have been much the poorer. At the stage of research, I was very much aided by Valeria Lovelace and Mary Smith at Children's Television Workshop; Midian Kurland, Jan Hawkins, Samuel Gibbon, Cynthia Char, and Karen Sheingold at the Bank Street Center for Children and Technology; James Levin, a pioneer researcher on children and computers, at the University of California, San Diego; Sherman Rosenfeld, a specialist in children's informal learning of science and technology; Oliver Moles at the National Institute of Education; and Thomas Malone at Xerox Palo Alto Research Center, author of the first experimental research on children and video games.

The fun in writing the book came from the many

people with whom I discussed it. I talked about the first draft with my neighbor and friend Andy Weiss, a filmmaker and student of the media, who responded not only with support but with provocative examples that became part of later drafts. While I was writing, Matthew was taking a ninth-grade English course that combined film with literature. This class, the students' response to it, and discussions with its inspiring and knowledgeable teacher, Jim Hosney (an instructor at the American Film Institute, as well as at Crossroads School), both confirmed and extended my ideas about the educational role of television and film. Conversations with Tom Baum, my old junior high classmate, now a Hollywood screenwriter, were stimulating and enjoyable. Winifred White, a member of NBC's children's programming department, gave me another perspective on children's television, as well as some very useful information.

Hilde Himmelweit, a pioneering researcher on children and television, gave me important guidance to the history of research in the area and to the British perspective on the subject. Mallory Wober, of England's Independent Broadcasting Authority, generously filled in the holes in my knowledge of British television by sending me material and answering questions. He also helped me to rethink some thorny problems.

Susan Chipman, from the National Institute of Education, gave a tough and very useful critique of my computer chapters and thoughtfully sent me written material with which to answer the questions she raised, all within some very unreasonable time constraints that I imposed. Karen Sheingold also was influential in modifying Chapter 8, both through making comments on the chapters and through sending me the latest unpublished reports from the Bank Street Center for Children and Technology. Gavriel Salomon commented on a chapter, sent me new and interesting material, and generously answered my questions about his work. Aimée Dorr provided hard-to-locate materials. Sylvia Scribner read the entire first draft; her comments simultaneously made me feel I was on the right track and provided extremely helpful suggestions for revision.

Jessica Beagles-Roos was my staunch colleague throughout the research on radio and television, which was supported by the National Institute of Education. She also read early drafts of several chapters and initiated and carried out data analysis that substantially modified Chapter 5. Wendy Weil, old friend, canoeing partner, and literary agent *par excellence*, gave me excellent advice at a number of crucial points. Paul Riskin skillfully did the computer printouts to illustrate the video game chapter. Richard Stengel came up with the book's title.

My parents, David and the late Doris Marks, supported me throughout the writing and commented on a number of chapters. My mother also served as a volunteer research assistant for my radio-television project, accurately coding large quantities of data.

Others who were generous in reading draft chapters were: Edward Palmer, Thomas Malone, Laurene Meringoff, Kathy Pezdek, Jerome Johnston, Gordon Berry, Sherman Rosenfeld, and my editors Eric Wanner, Helen Fraser, Barbara Lloyd, Jerome Bruner, and Michael Cole. In addition, Eric's positive feedback at the early stages and availability throughout gave me the courage and enthusiasm to complete the project. My manuscript editor, Camille Smith, managed to make the book accessible to more readers, despite working with a temperamental author who didn't like her baby undergoing major surgery.

My children, Lauren and Matthew, were tolerant of being neglected while I was in the throes of writing.

Even more, both helped with the project itself. Lauren took pictures for the book and did library work and errands, even when she didn't want to. Matthew showed me how to play video games, introduced me to interesting new ones, read chapters, put manuscript corrections on the computer, ran chapters through the proofreading program, assembled the software references, and helped with illustrations for the video game chapter. Most important, he was a constant source of moral support to the very end.

I would like to express my thanks and appreciation for all of these contributions. I hope that each person who helped will find satisfaction in the final outcome of all of our efforts.

P.M.G.

Contents

Credits

Mind and Media

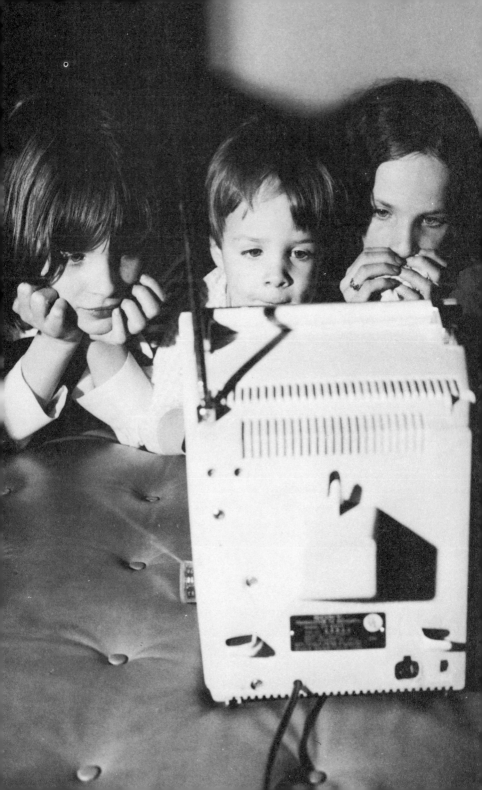

1 / The Electronic Media

In California there is a group called the Couch Potatoes, who consider themselves "the true televisionaries." They take their name from their favorite place for vegetating in front of the TV set, and from a vegetable with many eyes. An ad to recruit members for the group goes like this: "Do you enjoy excessive amounts of TV viewing? Were some of the most enjoyable times of your life experienced in front of your set? Were your formative years nurtured by the 'electronic babysitter'? Are you annoyed by crybaby intellectuals who claim that TV viewing is counterproductive and a waste of time? Like to do most of your living on the couch?"

Asked by a reporter to comment on a two-way cable TV system that allows viewers to talk back to the television, one of the Couch Potatoes responded: "Why watch TV if you have to think and respond? As far as I'm concerned, the main point of watching TV is that it lets you *avoid* having to do that. To put it another way, if you're going to have to respond to your TV, you might as well go out and cultivate friendships or read a book or something."[1]

The Couch Potatoes consciously caricature, by carrying to an absurd extreme, the idea that television is a passive, anti-intellectual medium, a medium that en-

1

courages people to vegetate. This opinion is shared by many others who consider the dangers of television too serious to make fun of. Falling scores on standardized tests, rising levels of violence in society, college students' inability to write well—these and other trends are blamed on the long hours recent generations of children have spent watching television.

In the past few years a new medium has come along to fascinate young people and worry their elders: video games. Some adults fear that, even more than television, the games are at best frivolous and at worst mindless, numbing, and violent. While many see the popularity of microcomputers among the young as a promising trend, others fear that they reinforce asocial or even antisocial tendencies.

My own opinion is that the damaging effects the electronic media can have on children are not intrinsic to the media but grow out of the ways the media are used. Much of the content of commercial TV shows may have a negative effect on children's social attitudes. Commercials themselves use sophisticated techniques to manipulate viewers into wanting certain products, and young children have no defenses against such techniques. And television watching *can* become a passive, deadening activity if adults do not guide their children's viewing and teach children to watch critically and to learn from what they watch.

But television and the newer electronic media, if used wisely, have great positive potential for learning and development. They give children different mental skills from those developed by reading and writing. Television is a better medium than the printed word for conveying certain types of information, and it makes learning available to groups of children who do not do well in traditional school situations—and even to people who cannot read. Video games introduce children to the world of microcomputers, at a time when computers are becoming increasingly important both in many jobs and in daily life. The interactive quality of both video games and computers forces children actively to create stimuli and information, not merely consume them.

The idea that television can be a positive force in children's lives has been around for decades. A classic study was done in England in the 1950s, when less than 10 percent of English families had TV sets and it was still possible to compare children who had television with children who did not. The authors suggested that parents and teachers inform themselves about television, not just to prevent children from seeing harmful programs, but to encourage them to watch worthwhile ones. They recommended discussing programs at home and in school, both to counteract one-sided views and to reinforce the impact of good programs. And they recommended teaching children critical viewing skills that would help them, for example, distinguish fantasy from reality. A study done in the United States a few years later emerged with many of the same suggestions.[2]

In the years since these early studies, television has become virtually universal in both Britain and the United States. Yet little progress has been made in using it positively, while awareness of its dangers has mushroomed. Much has been written about the negative effects of television on children: the titles of two popular and interesting books on the subject, *The Plug-In Drug* and *Four Arguments for the Elimination of Television*, carry the message.[3] But we do not have the option of getting rid of television. Television, video games, and other computer technology are here to stay, and their growing pervasiveness makes it all the more urgent that we discover how best to use them.

THE MESSAGE OF THE MEDIUM

Twenty years ago Marshall McLuhan advanced the revolutionary thesis that "the medium is the message."[4] His idea was that each medium of communication produces social and psychological effects on its audience, particular social relations and a particular form of consciousness or way of thinking, that are quite independent of the content being transmitted. These effects constitute the message of the medium. McLuhan's famous phrase is widely quoted (even if not widely understood). But his own work, consisting mainly of literary analysis and artistic intuition, provided more free-ranging speculation than scientifically grounded information about the nature of these effects. Moreover, two closely related media that are now of great and growing importance, video games and other uses of computer technology, did not exist as mass media at the time McLuhan wrote. Today, research into the effects of the media is a thriving field, but we are only beginning to understand from a scientific perspective what the media, from print and radio to television, video games, and computers, do to our consciousness.

In this book I attempt to spell out the message of each medium as it concerns children and their development. (Although its focus is children, the book is really about how all of us, children and adults, are socialized by the media. It concerns the media and *human*, not merely *child* development.) The largest number of pages is devoted to television, the medium with which children spend the largest number of hours. (In general, I include film as a subpart of television, rather than treating it as a separate medium.) Next in emphasis is computers— video games and other uses of computer technology. These media are too new to have been much studied. Whereas my analysis of the effects of television is supported by a large body of empirical data, the discussion of computer technology is necessarily more speculative.

Two other media, print and radio, are brought in mainly for comparative purposes. Print was the first mass medium historically, and it was closely tied to the rise of formal education. Radio was the second mass medium and is currently the major one in many Third World countries. In order to understand the psychological changes brought about by television, it is crucial to compare its effects with those of the media that preceded it.

For many people print is still the hallmark of education and the standard against which all other media tend to be measured. Those with this world view often perceive television, film, and the newer electronic media as a threat to print. In fact, however, each medium presents its own point of view on a subject.[5] It makes little sense to give one point of view a privileged status, as intellectuals and the educational establishment have done with print. As McLuhan puts it, "we have confused reason with literacy, and rationalism with a single technology."[6]

Although I have been socialized and educated mainly through print, my goal in this book is to maintain a balanced view of the various media, profiling the distinctive strengths and weaknesses of each as a means of communication and learning. Each medium has a contribution to make to human development. One medium's strength is another's weakness; thus the media are complementary, not in opposition. Balanced development requires a balanced diet composed of the various media. Growing up exposed to a variety of media, children may not emerge from their education as specialized for reading as they once were. But they will have a more diversified set of skills than was possible when print was the dominant mass medium.

As each new medium comes to prominence, the preceding ones tend to take on new functions or to become specialized in what they do best.[7] With the coming of television, radio became specialized for music. Reading has become more associated with education, while the reading of serious novels for pleasure has to some extent been supplanted by movies. It is time to consider whether print has not, in our educational system, been assigned tasks that other media can do better.

I do not want to give the impression of being a media Pollyanna. Each medium has problems as well as possibilities. Some children watch far too much television, and need to have their viewing restricted: in one experiment, cutting six-year-olds' normal viewing time caused shifts from a more impulsive to a more reflective intellectual style and produced increases in nonverbal IQ.[8] It is also important, for a number of reasons, to guide children away from violent programs.[9] Literacy is vital in modern society, and the newer media should not be allowed to take the place of reading and writing for our children. Learning is impossible without active participation and mental effort, so the passivity encouraged by television must be overcome if television is to be a tool for learning.

But such negative reactions, important as they are, have been heard many times before. The greater need is for positive ideas that can help make television and the newer electronic media constructive forces in children's lives. In this book I emphasize the potential of each medium rather than its most typical uses. I delineate the positive role each can have in an essentially multi-media world. For the most part, I do not seek solutions to problems of children and the media by suggesting improvements in the media themselves. While a number of such suggestions will be found throughout the book, my dominant emphasis is to pick out positive instances, positive effects, and constructive uses of each medium, alone and in combination. For the present this seems a practical approach, for the media themselves are generally beyond the control of individuals to change, and parents and teachers have to cope as best they can with the actual media environments available to children. Nevertheless, by calling attention to the positive aspects and uses of each medium as it now exists, I hope to contribute to an expansion of these positive practices and examples.

Properly used, every medium, without exception, can provide opportunities for human learning and development. The task now is to find a niche for each medium, so that each can contribute to a creative system of multimedia education.

2 / Film and Television Literacy

Children do not always understand film or television the same way adults do. A friend of mine remembers his early misinterpretation of television: he thought that if he changed channels he would see different parts of the same character's body. For example, if a character's head was on the screen, he thought he could find the feet on another channel. To him, the screen was a real-world space, and everything happening in this same real-world space was surely related. This same friend tells of overhearing a child, about age 3, at the film *E.T.* Whenever the character Elliot was off-screen, the boy would ask, "Where's Elliot, Dad? Where's Elliot?" He did not realize that a given shot merely *samples* the world of a film: that a character can be off-camera and still be alive and well in the film.

As these anecdotes illustrate, our understanding of film or television depends upon knowing the medium's symbolic code. For example, if Image A and Image B alternate on the screen in progressively shorter and quicker fragments (a technique known as accelerated montage), an experienced moviegoer, one familiar with the code, will get the message that A and B exist at the same time but in separate spaces, and that they are converging on each other either spatially or dramati-

9

cally. Learning to decode the symbols of film or television is something like learning to read. The skills it requires are not as specialized as those needed for reading, but they are nevertheless considerable. By metaphoric extension from the medium of print, I shall refer to knowledge of this audiovisual code as television (or film) literacy. (Because television and film use the same basic code and because films appear on television, I treat them in this book as equivalent, although some theorists, notably Marshall McLuhan, emphasize their differences. Most often I use the term television literacy, with the understanding that it includes film literacy.)

Some of the elements a television viewer must decode are visual, generated by techniques such as cutting from one shot to another, panning the camera from one side of a scene to another, zooming from long shot to close-up, splitting the screen. Others are auditory, such as faceless narrators or canned laughter. Each of these techniques is a form of symbolic representation, that is, each technique stands for something in the real world. For example, when a camera zooms in on a detail it communicates a relationship between that detail and its larger context. A simple cut usually means a change of perspective on a given scene. A dissolve (where one shot visually dissolves into another) signifies a change of scene or a change of time. Split screen denotes an act of comparison. The use of a faceless narrator implies that the person narrating has some distance, either physical or psychological, from the scene being portrayed. Symbolic conventions like these, taken together, form a code the viewer must know in order to comprehend what happens on the screen.[1]

One reason children sometimes misunderstand film or television is that they do not always know how to interpret the relationships between shots. (A shot is a sequence in which the camera is continuously on.) These relationships usually carry information about space and time; for example, two successive shots can represent a change of scene or two points of view on the same scene. Visual signals separating large film units, such as dissolves or fades (where one shot gradually fades into or out of black) serve as punctuation, giving cues as to how the shots are interrelated.[2] The ability to understand such interrelationships partly depends on a child's stage of development. There is evidence that children cannot correctly infer relationships among scenes in adult TV shows until some time after age seven. Younger children tend to treat each shot as an independent entity. Many young children do not even use the *order* of shots in interpreting a dramatic program; thus their memories of the program have a fragmented quality.[3]

Recent research in the United States indicates that the ability to interpret a sequence of shots does exist to some extent at younger ages. After watching a puppet film made especially for children, only thirty seconds long, and with a familiar theme, even three- and five-year-olds could act out the film using the same puppets that appeared in the film, and their reconstructions were just as accurate when the film consisted of separate shots as when it consisted of one thirty-second shot.[4] Thus, children between ages three and five in the TV-saturated United States have a rudimentary knowledge of interrelations between shots that they can apply to material at their own level, but they are unable to comprehend the connections in adult shows (which they nevertheless love to watch). The growth of this skill is a developmental process not complete before age ten.[5]

Even after children have the basic idea of interrelating shots, particular methods (what film-makers call techniques of montage) can still confuse them. In a second study using short puppet films, more than 80 percent of the four-year-olds correctly reenacted action that was portrayed in a single shot without the use of montage techniques, but almost half did not understand accelerated montage, in which alternating shots depict a simultaneous time relation. Such inferences about time seemed particularly difficult. Inferences about character perspective—what someone is seeing or thinking—were somewhat easier: about 60 percent of the four-year-olds understood a technique to show character perspective by placing the camera where the character would be and using voiceover to present the character's voice.

The four-year-olds had no trouble understanding ellipsis, in which two parts of an action are shown with a gap between and the viewer must mentally fill in the gap. The relative ease of interpreting this technique may derive from the fact that, developmentally, comprehension of action precedes understanding of time or the perspective of another person. Reconstructing space, either from a succession of shots, from camera movement, or from partial view, was of intermediate difficulty, about the same as character perspective. Understanding of all techniques improved with age.[6]

Lack of understanding of montage techniques can lead to dramatic misunderstanding. In Germany, some six-year-olds thought the hero in a televised version of *Town and Country Mouse* was a different, older mouse in close-up than in long shot. When African adults who lacked experience with film and photographs were shown films about insect pests, they expressed pleasure that they did not have insects as large as those depicted in close-up shots.[7] Evidently specific experience with the code of film, as well as a certain stage of cognitive development, is necessary for understanding the symbols used in television and film.

In Israel, Gavriel Salomon and Akiba Cohen studied the understanding of montage techniques in ten-year-olds, using five versions of an eight-minute film. One version was based on the fragmentation of space: shots were taken from different points of view, so that the viewer had to interrelate fragmented spaces to follow the plot. Another version contained logical gaps: segments of some scenes were deleted, creating brief breaks in continuity. A third version was made up of numerous close-ups interspersed with long shots; a fourth of many zoom-ins and zoom-outs. The fifth version was as simple and straightforward as possible.

Children remembered the straightforward film better than any version that required them to construct a causal or spatial relationship between shots. Only the zoom version was understood virtually as well as the straightforward version.[8] A zoom is a single shot, and therefore does not require the viewer to infer a relation between shots. This work confirms the American research with younger children on two important points: an understanding of visual techniques cannot be taken for granted, and the use of these techniques affects how well a film will be understood.

The Israeli researchers asked another question: Does a child's ability to interpret the visual techniques of film depend on more general visual skills? Children were tested on skills related to the editing techniques used in the different versions of the film. One of these tests, the Space Construction Task (see figure 1), asked the child to put four pictures together to form a whole. This corresponds to a technique in which camera shots of parts of some scene must be integrated mentally to construct an image of the whole.

All versions of the film except the straightforward one required the child to coordinate bits of spatial information. Not surprisingly, success on the Space Construction Task was correlated with comprehension of

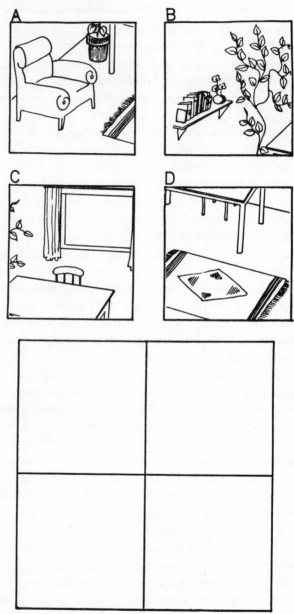

1. *An item from the Space Construction Test. (From Salomon,* Interaction of Media, Cognition, and Learning.)

all the versions of the film except the straightforward one: the better a child did on the Space Construction Task, the better he or she understood the more highly edited films. This outcome implies that comprehension of film, with its symbolic devices, is related to more general visual skills.

ACQUIRING TELEVISION LITERACY

It is very difficult to separate the effects of maturation, general experience, and specific experience with television on the growth of TV literacy skills. By working in Israel, a country with much less television than the United States, Salomon was able to gain some insight into the impact of television-watching experience on these skills. In a sense, his work tests the very idea of TV literacy: Is TV literacy acquired through experience with the medium, as print literacy is?

Sesame Street was introduced to Israel in 1971. At that time Israel was what Salomon calls TV naive: there was only one channel, which had been introduced three years earlier, and it broadcast only four hours a night, of which only half an hour was children's programming. The style of *Sesame Street*, based on the kaleidoscope format of American commercials, was totally novel.

Besides examining the impact of *Sesame Street* on the acquisition of specific knowledge, such as knowledge of the alphabet, Salomon designed tests to measure skills related to the program's code of symbolic representation.[9] An example from one test is shown in figure 2. Success at this task involves understanding a shift in visual point of view and being able to imagine a point of view different from one's own. This test is related to the production technique of showing the same object or person from different camera angles. The idea was that

Imagine that you are the girl sitting on the window sill. How would you see the painter?

2. *An item from the Test of Changing Points of View.* (*From Salomon, Interaction of Media, Cognition, and Learning.*)

children's performance on the test would be improved by experience in watching TV scenes using this technique.

Among seven- to nine-year-olds, heavy viewers of *Sesame Street* did significantly better on all the tests, and this result held for both middle-class and working-class children. In other words, children who watched a lot of this program, whatever their social class, were acquiring specific TV literacy skills, such as understanding the meaning of a close-up. Television literacy is indeed fostered by exposure to television itself.

The children with the highest TV literacy skills also had the greatest knowledge of the show's content. Content in *Sesame Street* means learning numbers, letters, and so forth. In fact, having good TV literacy skills at one time made it easier for children to learn the content taught by the program at a later time. The opposite effect did not occur, however; learning cognitive content did not influence the later acquisition of TV literacy skills. This finding has application to learning in school as well as out, and to older students as well as young children. For example, in a high school physics class that included a series of films, students with more experience with films in general learned more from the physics films. It seems that the value of film as an educational medium depends on the level of film literacy students bring to it.[10]

Thus television literacy, developed partly through exposure to television, partly through development, makes it possible to use television to transmit knowledge and cognitive skills to the young child. The parallel to print is clear: the acquisition of basic literacy skills make it possible to use print to transmit information and ideas. There is a difference, however: children must be *taught* to read, but they learn TV literacy on their own by simply watching television.

Salomon has also experimented with using television to cultivate children's more general visual skills. Many of the techniques of television make relationships visible that would otherwise have to be constructed in a person's head. For example, when a camera zooms in on a detail, this makes the relationship between a part and its whole visually explicit. Salomon investigated whether use of the zoom technique to highlight details could help eighth-grade children to single out details from a complex visual display that was not televised.[11] He showed one group of children films of a painting, in which the camera zoomed in on details and out again to the entire painting eighty times. Another group simply practiced identifying details from a slide of a painting. Both before and after this training the children were tested by being asked to pick out as many details as possible from a slide of a classroom scene.

Salomon found that the benefit of the zoom training depended on the child's initial level of visual skill. Children who began with low ability to notice details benefited much more from the zoom training than from simple practice. But children who were already skilled in noticing visual detail actually did slightly worse after the zoom experience; for them, simple practice without the zoom was most helpful.

Thus, the value of the zoom technique in teaching children the relationship between a detail and its whole seemed greater at the early stages of learning. At a certain level of skill, the more challenging task of picking out details without the aid of the camera became the best way of perfecting the skill. The same pattern of results emerged with other camera techniques. It seems that camera techniques can promote the learning of visual skills. But in modeling visual processes the camera partially takes over from the viewer. It can thus do *too* much for a viewer who already has the basic skills. At that point, further development demands a more independent and active form of practice.

USING TELEVISION FORMS AND FORMATS TO IMPROVE LEARNING

Some features of television attract the attention of young children more than others do. For example, action and sound effects are more attention-getting than dialogue. The use of these features to highlight the important points in a television narrative makes those points more understandable to five- and six-year-olds. By age eight, the attention-getting devices become unnecessary; comprehension is good with or without them.[12] A given TV show or type of show may develop its own special symbolic devices, called formats, and familiarity with the format may help children learn new material from the show. For example, *Sesame Street* has a sorting format: four objects appear on the screen, three of which are identical; the fourth is different in some way. Along with this display goes a song that begins, "One of these things is not like the others."[13] The idea is that once a child learns the format, the format can help the child learn more complex ways of sorting items.

Programs from Children's Television Workshop use recurrent formats to get the child actively involved through anticipating what comes next. In an example from *The Electric Company*, the camera focuses on street signs, as if the viewer were riding in a car and reading them. Meanwhile a song gives the name of each sign as the camera focuses on it. Then the "car ride" is repeated with the music only, inviting the child to fill in the words.[14] In this way, a symbolic form goes beyond transmitting meaning and induces children to create it for themselves.

KNOWING MORE COMPLEX FORMATS

Some older children and adults can switch on a television program in the middle and reconstruct what has happened up to that point. To my knowledge, no research exists on this subject; but it seems to me that these are people who have become familiar with conventional formats on a more complex level than those in children's programs—perhaps the format of the Western or the spy story or a particular situation comedy. Experience with the format then serves as an aid in understanding and even reconstructing content.

One complex format is that of *Hill Street Blues*, a very popular American police show with multiple subplots. Film and television are able to depict many things happening at once, in contrast with print and radio, which are limited to depicting one thing at a time. During scenes at the police station in *Hill Street Blues*, a single shot will show many people carrying out various activities relating to several subplots. I watched *Hill Street Blues* once and found it impossible to follow. I kept looking for a single thread to focus on in these complex scenes. The teenagers with whom I was watching had no difficulty whatsoever, and at least one of them had not been following the show regularly. Clearly they understood the multiple-subplot format and could use it to interpret complex scenes.

Psychology makes the distinction between parallel processing, in which a person takes in multiple pieces of information simultaneously, and serial processing, in which a person processes one item at a time. A complex picture tends to elicit parallel processing, while words elicit serial processing. It seems to me likely that watching television, in contrast to reading, cultivates parallel processing as strategy for taking in information. Comprehension of a show like *Hill Street Blues* would seem to require and encourage this strategy.

Knowledge of complex formats has value for predicting as well as for understanding. Television-literate people often know what is going to happen next in a film or TV program. Watching a new police drama with my thirteen-year-old son, Matthew, I expressed amazement when the police officer's own daughter turned out to be the culprit. Matthew responded, "It has to be his daughter. That's how all these police shows work. Everything is interconnected." Not only is Matthew able to predict, but he bases his prediction on awareness of a recurrent plot format.

Steven Spielberg, a member of the first generation of movie directors who grew up watching television, has begun to take this sophistication of his audience into account. In an interview following the release of *E.T.* and *Poltergeist*, Spielberg said that after a given shot he tries to keep the audience off balance for the next two, instead of giving them what they expect. He does not want his audience to be able to predict his films too well. Implicit in his remark is the idea that they *will* predict if the format is too conventional. Spielberg remarked about making an earlier film, *Raiders of the Lost Ark*, that because audiences are sophisticated about film, making a movie is like "some kind of kinetic chess—if you don't stay five moves ahead of them, you're dead."[15] It may be partly this transcendence of the conventional formats now mastered by experienced film audiences that makes Spielberg's films so popular.

The idea of television or film literacy may be agreeable to many people because it implies that, mentally, they are doing more than vegetating when they sit in front of the television set. It may be comforting to parents in particular to think that, while perhaps less literate than they would like in the print medium, their children are acquiring literacy skills in the domain of television. There *is* a mental challenge to television, although, unlike the case with reading, the challenge can be met without special instruction. Nevertheless, experience with the medium is required to master the code of television.

Although the code of television is complex and varied, there is a danger that it will be used automatically and without effort: that the symbolic code of television will be processed passively rather than actively. This problem cannot be solved on the level of the code itself. It is a question of attitudes toward television and of the web of social interaction in which television or film viewing takes place. This crucial problem of how to turn automatic processing of a code into active mental involvement with a medium will be discussed in later chapters.

3 / Television and Learning

Part of the message of a medium, as we have seen, lies in the information-processing skills fostered by its technology, forms, and code. Another part of a medium's message, also created by its forms and technology, is its bias toward presenting certain types of information rather than others. The fact that television's images are both visual and moving makes it particularly well suited to present two particular kinds of content: information about dynamic processes of action and transformation, and information about space. The predominance of visual motion also suits television to the mental abilities of the young child.

MOTION AND LEARNING

The characteristic that sets television and film apart from earlier media is visual movement. Movement can help children learn, because, first, it attracts their attention to the screen. In Sweden, for example, where narrated stills are used for young children's television in a picture-book format, children say they prefer movement, making comments like "It's no fun unless it moves!"[1]

A second way visual movement aids learning is by

making information about action easier to remember. Elementary school children recall actions from a narrated television story better than they recall actions from the same story read to them from a picture book. The TV version makes these actions visually explicit, whereas in the picture-book version they are visually implicit, although they may be described verbally in the narration. The children who watch the TV version also use action more in later reasoning about the story.[2]

This ability of film or television to teach about actions can have useful applications. Actions are very much involved in manual and physical skills. In England, filmed motion was compared with still pictures as a way to teach children ages four to eight how to put together a complex wooden puzzle.[3] While the still pictures did help some (in comparison with no instruction), the filmed demonstration led to the greatest success with the task. The visual movement intrinsic to television and film makes these media well suited to teach tasks involving physical skill.

This characteristic of television is also useful in teaching about topics that emphasize dynamic processes rather than static states. One example comes from Sweden. Five- and seven-year-olds watched films about the process of a tree going *From Seed to Telephone Pole*.[4] One group saw an animated narrated film, the other a narrated film made up of still pictures. Children of both ages learned more information from the animated version.

For the seven-year-olds, the advantage of motion was in teaching about the dynamic processes presented in the film. The animated film showed the seed sprouting its roots, for example, while the still version merely included pictures of the seed without and then with roots (see figure 3). Even though the narrator of both versions described the action explicitly—"Suddenly, a little root

3. *"Suddenly a little root breaks through the shell of the seed."* (Adapted from Rydin, "Children's Understanding of Television.")

breaks through the shell of the seed"—seven-year-olds who saw the animated film remembered this fact better than those who saw the still version. It seems clear that motion made the growth process more explicit and understandable.

The five-year-olds also learned better from the animated film, but for them the advantage was not in learning about particular processes. At this age, motion seemed primarily to stimulate attention; even motion that was irrelevant to the film's content improved their learning.

It seems likely that the reason animation did not help the younger children to learn about the processes is that they were preoperational: that is, they had not yet reached Piaget's stage of concrete operations, a stage characterized by a relatively mature understanding of physical transformations. By age seven, when children typically have attained this stage, they are better able to learn about physical processes from film.

A study of children's reactions to the popular American series *The Incredible Hulk* shows how preoperational children can misunderstand a visible transformation portrayed on television. Most of the time, the hero of the show, David Banner, looks and acts like a normal person, but when he gets angry he turns, on screen, into an ugly, green-faced monster. The two forms of the character are played by different actors, but the film is edited to imply that the hero is transformed into the Hulk right before the viewers' eyes. Children between the ages of three and five tend to see the character's two forms as separate people. In contrast, nine-through-eleven-year-olds, who have reached the stage of concrete operations, generally see David and the Hulk as one character.[5] It seems that children's ability to learn about or understand processes of transformation from television is limited by their stage of cognitive development.

tracks were identical in both versions.) The advantage of television over radio was larger for the younger children and for the harder problems. At kindergarten age children apparently are ready to begin to solve this type of spatial problem, but only with the aid of visual cues such as those provided by television. Later there comes a point when the child is able to solve such problems without the visual cues. This experiment shows that television can help a child learn by demonstrating a spatial relationship that the child cannot yet construct from purely verbal information. It reinforces the value of television for modeling a visual/spatial skill at an early stage of learning, a point that emerged in the last chapter.

MAKING TELEVISION FIT THE CHILD

Sesame Street shows how scientific knowledge about the ways children think and learn at certain ages can be applied to creating an educational program for children. Let me give a few examples.[7] First, the creators of *Sesame Street* wanted to determine what attracted the attention of their potential audience and to emphasize these elements in the program. Examples of such elements are animation, puppets, and sound effects. Second, *Sesame Street* made use of a Piagetian principle of knowledge acquisition that applies to all ages: to learn something new, you generally need to be able to relate it to something you already know. Thus, to teach letter shapes, segments would start with a familiar object having the same shape as the letter being taught. Y, for example, might be compared with a fork in the road. Third, *Sesame Street* used the principle that repetition enhances learning. Testing a segment designed to teach recognition of the letter J, the researchers found that more children

Motion attracts the child's attention; it helps child[ren] remember the action of a story; it can help children [of] the right age learn about processes; and it can aid in t[he] teaching of physical skills. The contexts in which the[se] different applications are and could be made are of cour[se] quite different. The tendency to acquire information abo[ut] actions in general is most relevant to entertainment pr[o]gramming. The advantages of using film to teach abou[t] biological or physical processes can be applied in do[c]umentary or instructional television or film. The abilit[y] to teach physical skills is useful in teaching trades, crafts, or sports.

SPATIAL SKILLS

Spatial skills are another type of skill that one might expect children to acquire from watching television. In discussing television literacy, I mentioned that certain spatial skills are required to interpret some of television's visual techniques. For instance, the skill of integrating different visual perspectives is necessary to interpret shots taken from different angles.

A Swiss study was designed to test the effectiveness of television in teaching children spatial information. Kindergarten and first-grade children saw or heard a television or radio version of a story.[6] In the story, the main characters, three children, were faced with some spatial problems. For example, they were going to see an owl, and they wanted the owl to think there was only one of them. To solve this problem, they walked in a line, with the tallest child first, so that the shorte[r] children were blocked from the owl's view. After seein[g] or hearing this story, each child was asked to act ou[t] the solutions to the problems, using puppets. More chil[d]ren could solve the problems after seeing the story o[n] television than after hearing it on the radio. (The soun[d] learned the letter after seeing the segment several times than after seeing it once.

The show also uses repetition to get children to participate actively, because active involvement is generally necessary for learning. For example, in one segment the actor James Earl Jones recites the alphabet, and each letter appears next to his head a moment before he says it. The first time through, the child says the letters along with Jones. After a few repetitions, the child starts to anticipate Jones, saying each letter after it appears on the screen but before Jones recites it. With still more repetition, the child names the letter *before* it appears. The anticipation elicited by repetition enables the child to learn the alphabet as well as to recognize the individual letters.

This example illustrates how television, even though it is a one-way medium, can be used to make the child an active participant. Observations of four-year-olds watching *Sesame Street* proved that the show also elicits, in most children, other types of activity, such as imitating verbal or physical action that has taken place on the show.[8]

The importance of activity to learning is not special to learning from television; it applies to all sorts of learning. Turning television from a passive to an active medium is central to exploiting its teaching potential. Much discussion in this book will focus on eliciting activity through forces outside the program itself, such as parent-child discussion. But *Sesame Street* makes the important point that through the judicious use of carefully chosen techniques television can, on its own, make the child an active participant.

In England, children's programs made by the BBC were attempting to get children to participate many years before *Sesame Street*. An example for preschool children is *Playschool*, which started in 1964. Later series on both public and commercial television (such as *You and Me* and *Mr. Trimble*) followed in the same tradition. The types of activity and the techniques used to elicit them are rather different from those used on *Sesame Street*. As one example, the host of a program may ask direct questions of the viewing child. In a second major type, the host presents ideas for games to play and things to make. These are basically the same techniques a nursery school teacher might use. However, in contrast to the response of the viewers of *Sesame Street*, preschool children rarely respond to the questions or carry out the suggested activities presented on these programs.[9] (In the United States, *Mr. Rogers* does get children to answer questions, perhaps by giving them plenty of time to respond.) As far as activities are concerned, it is hard to participate in a game or to make something while watching a program at the same time. Nursery school techniques may lose their effectiveness when transferred to television. It may be that the methods used by *Sesame Street*, which stimulate mental rather than physical activity, and do so by format rather than by request, succeed better because they are better suited to the medium of television.

The English children studied do sometimes carry out activities stimulated by a television program. But they do so *after* rather than *while* watching, and their mothers play a key role; the stimulus of television is not enough.[10] Such activities seem to require an adult to use the television for the child, a theme to which I shall return later.

The contrast between children's observed responses to *Sesame Street* and to the British shows suggests that the ways of getting children to participate actively cannot simply be transferred from earlier forms of communication. Nevertheless, some British shows, such as *You and Me*, do stimulate impressive learning even without overt activity on the part of the viewers.[11]

A PARADOX

There is a paradox in this chapter. In my discussion of the potential of television to aid learning, virtually all of the positive examples come from experimental films and programming made for educational television. Certainly one implication is that adults need to see that children view these sorts of programs. However, we must also face the fact that the average child does not spend very much time with this type of fare. Instead, children spend long hours watching adult films, comedies, and action adventures.[12] Is the learning potential I have discussed actually available to them?

A number of the formal features I have discussed are intrinsic to all television, not just to experimental or educational programs. This is true of both motion and space. My hypothesis is that children learn to assimilate information about action, process, and physical transformation through their expsure to all sorts of television and film. In the same way, I think it likely that children get information about the two-dimensional representation of three-dimensional space through many types of programs. These are the messages of the medium: effects on thinking that are produced by the technology and the forms, rather than by any particular content.

I do not think that these possible benefits should be a rationalization for too many hours spent with entertainment programming. Far better to receive television's cognitive messages through a TV diet that includes some mind-stretching programs while avoiding harmful content. These issues will be discussed in Chapters 4 and 9. Nor should too many hours be spent with television in general, no matter how worthy the content. As a medium, television has its strengths, but it also has its weaknesses. Such weaknesses as the passivity of the viewer and the lack of opportunity to use the imagination will also be taken up in later chapters, where I will show that the weaknesses of television are strengths of other media. Balanced development for a child requires not only the skills and qualities developed by television but those fostered by other media of communication as well.

4 / Television and Social Reality

As a parent, I have feared both that my children were *not* learning from television and that they were. On the one hand, it is only natural to want your children to get something constructive out of the long hours spent in front of the television. On the other hand, I have serious doubts about the content of many programs and therefore hope that the children have not absorbed it. Many of my fears center on television's messages about the nature of the social world: what different kinds of people are like and how they act toward each other. Some parents may feel more in harmony with the social reality that is projected on television than I do. Television in other countries may be presenting different views of the social world. In many countries, the issue may be the importation of a foreign social reality that comes with buying American or British television. In order to cope with any of these situations, it is important to know how children interpret and use the social messages presented on television.

SEX-ROLE STEREOTYPES

The evidence overwhelmingly indicates that television does influence children's views of social reality.[1]

One effect it can have is to encourage stereotyped opinions about social topics such as sex roles. Content analysis of TV programming in the United States has shown that television generally presents highly stereotyped views of male and, particularly, female roles, and studies indicate that, as early as age three, heavy television viewers in the United States have more stereotyped views of sex roles than do light viewers.[2] Children simply learn what is presented on U.S. television—sex role stereotypes. The conclusions of George Gerbner, a pioneer in the analysis of the social world portrayed on U.S. television, have been summarized this way: "Male prime-time characters out-number females by 3 to 1 and, with a few exceptions, women are portrayed as weak, passive satellites to powerful effective men. TV's male population also plays a vast variety of roles, while females generally get typecast as either lovers or mothers. Less than 20% of TV's married women with children work outside the home—as compared with more than 50% in real life."[3] Analysis of British television yields the same conclusions.[4]

Commercials are outstanding culprits in the presentation of sex role stereotypes. In an experiment, one group of high school girls was shown fifteen commercials emphasizing the importance of physical beauty, while another group was not shown the commercials. The girls who watched the commercials were more likely than the others to agree with the statements "beauty is personally desirable for me" and "beauty is important to be popular with men."[5] However, to put this effect in perspective, it should be noted that television, even without commercials (for example, in Britain twenty-five years ago and in Sweden today), influences children to attach more importance to appearance in general and clothes in particular.[6] This seems to be the effect of television being a visual medium, even without any effort to sell physical beauty.

It is not just beauty commercials that use sexual stereotypes to sell products. Researchers at the University of Kansas have investigated what clusters of features commercials associate with toys intended for boys versus those intended for girls. Commercials for girls' toys contain more fades, dissolves, and background music; those for boys' toys contain more toy action, frequent cuts, sound effects, and loud music. The researchers created pseudo-commercials consisting of abstract shapes rather than real toys and containing one or the other of these clusters of features and showed them to children of various ages. Children of all ages tended to identify the features from commercials for girls' toys as female and those from commercials for boys' toys as male, and this identification got stronger with age.[7] This is an example of the way recurrent formats, which I discussed in Chapter 2, set up expectations that affect children's response to new material. In this instance, the format is being used to track girls toward certain types of merchandise, boys toward other types, without ever bringing the message of sex-typing to the level of explicit verbal awareness.

Television can do more than reinforce stereotypes. It is so powerful a medium that with careful planning it can also be used to break down social stereotypes. The best example here is *Freestyle*, a series produced for U.S. public television with the express purpose of changing sex-role attitudes in nine- through twelve-year-old children. In thirteen half-hour segments, the show presented dramatized vignettes in which girls came to see that they could be independent and career-minded in traditionally male fields, and in which boys learned to be nurturant and to express emotions. The goal was to produce more acceptance of and interest in nontraditional work and family roles, such as scientific, mechanical, and athletic activities for girls, nurturant activities for boys.[8]

The series was successful in a number of respects. First of all, it attracted an audience. According to Nielsen ratings, it was watched in 1,640,000 homes. Although this was only 5.5 percent of households with children aged six to eleven, the absolute numbers indicate television's impressive ability to reach people.

To test the effects of *Freestyle*, researchers studied more than seven thousand children in seven U.S. cities. Some of the children watched the show at home; each week their teachers reminded them to do so. Others viewed the show in their classrooms. For still others, teachers introduced each episode and followed it up with class discussion and activities drawn from a teacher's guide.

The children who watched at home saw the show much less often than the other groups (although much more often than if they had not been encouraged by their teachers). Not surprisingly, the effects were smallest in this group. The show had a stronger effect on the group that viewed the program at school; for instance, more children came to believe that husbands are capable of doing housework and that traditionally female jobs such as secretary and nurse are held by men as well as women. While the effects of simply viewing *Freestyle* were already considerable, they were both intensified and expanded when the show was discussed in class. For example, just watching the show convinced female students that it is good for boys to assume helping roles like housework and child care; but it took classroom discussion to convince male students.

The experience of *Freestyle* indicates the potential, thus far exploited only to a very limited degree in the United States, for using television to help children expand their image of different groups in society. It also points up the capacity for classroom discussion to magnify the learning impact of a television program; and it demonstrates the benefits of bringing television into the classroom. The overwhelming majority of teachers were enthusiastic about using the program in their classes. This reaction is one indication that it is indeed feasible to integrate television in the school curriculum.

It is a sad commentary on the U.S. system of support for broadcasting that *Freestyle*, a program that has proved its value in both systematic research and audience interest, has not been continued in production and is, as of now, being broadcast in only one city in the United States, Pittsburgh. At the same time, children are being exposed every day to a heavy diet of sex-role stereotypes on commercial television.

Not all commercial TV shows portray sex-role stereotypes; the right kind of commercial programming can counter such stereotypes. An experimental study was done involving *All in the Family*, an adult comedy series that also attracted a large audience among children.[9] The central character, Archie Bunker, is a very opinionated, traditional, and prejudiced working-class man. The study used an episode about some neighbors of the Bunkers who had nontraditional sex roles: Frank, the husband, did the cooking; Irene, the wife, fixed household appliances. Children between the ages of five and eleven watched the show in small groups and were interviewed about sex-role concepts before and after viewing. Above age five, children decreased their stereotyping as a result of seeing the program. This effect was larger if an adult made comments about the program during natural pauses, such as "Look, Irene fixed Edith's mixer all by herself" or "There's Frank cooking. He seems to really like cooking."

Two important facts emerge from this study. First,

with the right content, a humorous, entertaining, and adult program can effectively counter the prevailing view of the social world presented on U.S. commercial television. Second, commentary on a program by an adult can magnify impact of the program on the child. These are the same basic points that emerged from the study of *Freestyle*. An important implication of this investigation of *All in the Family* is that education is not limited to educational programming; entertainment programming can also educate in important ways.

A similar study was done in England with a children's show called *Rainbow*.[10] Like the *All in the Family* episode, the *Rainbow* show presented a story that included a family in which traditional sex roles were reversed. As in the U.S. study, viewing the program moved attitudes toward less traditional sex role concepts, particularly increased acceptance of male participation in housework.

However, as attitudes solidify with age, such changes become more difficult to bring about. Prejudiced adults identify with and find support for their views in Archie Bunker, the bigot, while liberals see the series as an exposé of prejudiced thinking.[11] For adults, *All in the Family* confirms preexisting attitudes, no matter what these are; the show's power to influence its audience in a new direction seems lost.

MINORITY GROUPS

Several studies have shown that TV can be used to enhance the self-respect of children who are members of an oppressed group. For example, research on *Sesame Street*, which portrays characters from various minority groups in a positive, nonstereotyped way, showed that minority children who watched the program gained in cultural pride, self-confidence, and interpersonal cooperation.[12] Television may also have a positive effect on the way members of disadvantaged groups are viewed by members of the advantaged majority. After watching *Sesame Street* for two years, white children in the United States developed more positive views toward children of other races; in Canada, special multiracial inserts added to regular *Sesame Street* shows have had a similar effect.[13]

Television in the United States usually portrays members of racial minorities as less powerful and poorer than the majority.[14] Every day, as both minority and majority children digest the typical American television fare, the image of minorities as relatively powerless and poor becomes internalized by children of all groups. In accord with the general principle that children identify with powerful figures rather than with powerless ones, black children often model themselves after white rather than black characters in a show.[15] This process, occurring in a racist society, can cause an identity conflict: how to have the status of a white person without ceasing to identify psychologically with one's own group? Television did not create this psychological problem, which stems from the oppression of minority groups. But by presenting an image of different groups in society that reflects the status quo, television helps to perpetuate this identity problem for minority children.

Disabled children make up another type of disadvantaged group whose self-image is affected by television. In Sweden a number of children's programs for and about deaf and hard-of-hearing children were produced. After watching these shows, "children with normal hearing acquired a keen interest in deaf and hard-of-hearing children, and a greater understanding of them, and they found it exciting to try to express themselves in the deaf children's secret sign language. The self-confidence of the deaf and hard-of-hearing children increased noticeably, in that they received appreciative attention from other children, saw others in the same situation as their own, and suddenly could understand the programs better." In the United States, *Sesame Street* has also produced benefits by presenting handicapped children in a realistic and positive light.[16]

Television can be a powerful tool for improving children's images of the groups that make up a pluralistic society. We have the choice of using the medium in this way or using it to reinforce negative stereotypes, as is far too often the case in current programming in the United States.

IMAGES OF OTHER COUNTRIES

The power of television can also be used to give children a positive image of life in other parts of the world. In the United States, ITT produced a series called *The Big Blue Marble*, aimed at children from eight to fourteen and designed to show positive attributes of children around the world. In an investigation of the program's effects, children were tested before and after viewing four episodes. After watching the episodes, children saw children in other countries as happier and better off, and were less likely to say that children from their own country were more fun, more interesting, more intelligent, and so forth. They also saw more similarity in people around the world. *The Big Blue Marble* also led to the world's largest pen pal program, a real-world testimony to the program's effects.[17]

Similar reductions in ethnocentric attitudes were observed in England twenty-five years ago when the BBC produced programs such as *Children's International Newsreel*, designed to inform children about other countries.[18] The reduction of national ethnocentrism is of great importance as the fate of one country becomes ever more interconnected with that of others. The communications revolution has been one factor in turning our planet into what McLuhan termed "the global village." We can enhance the chances for survival of that village by using the media of communication, such as television, to improve our information about other countries, thus reducing dangerous stereotypes and international paranoia. What better place to start than, as *The Big Blue Marble* did, with children? Because of ITT's long-term support, *The Big Blue Marble* is now one of the most widely syndicated programs, seen in sixty-three countries.

THE IMPACT OF A SINGLE MOVIE

Film resembles television in having a powerful effect on children's view of the social world. Fifty years ago, long before television, a program of research known as the Payne Fund Studies focused on the effect of movies on preadolescent and adolescent students. R. C. Peterson and L. L. Thurstone, the authors of one of the Payne Fund volumes, selected thirteen feature films they thought might influence social attitudes: for example, *The Birth of a Nation* was expected to influence racial attitudes; *All Quiet on the Western Front*, attitudes toward war. The researchers tested children's attitudes before and after each film. (The children were white students from small midwestern towns.)[19]

About half the films produced a shift in attitudes after one viewing, and in some cases the shifts were very large. For example, before seeing *The Birth of a Nation*, about 80 percent of the students had scores of 8 or over on a scale of attitudes toward blacks (where 11 represented the most positive attitude on the scale). After seeing the film, only about 45 percent had scores in this range. Five months later, the students' racial attitudes were still more negative than they had been before the film, although the effect of the film had decayed over time. In general, long-term effects were about midway between the original attitudes and the attitudes right after the film. Effects lasted as long as nineteen months, the longest interval tested. Another important finding was that these effects were cumulative; seeing two or three films with a consistent position on a given topic caused more change in attitudes than seeing a single film.

This study indicates that a single exposure to a powerful film can have a definite impact on a young person's view of the world. Film has had a special impact on American culture; especially before the coming of television, people all over the country would see the same films. Even today, many more children view a popular film than see almost any given television show. Thus, any effect of a popular film is a mass effect.

An interesting question is why only half the films produced changes in attitudes. Because the most renowned film, *The Birth of a Nation*, produced the largest effect and because those films which did not change attitudes are unknown today, I would speculate that the power to influence social attitudes depends on the artistic and dramatic quality of the film. This is an issue that bears further investigation.

The finding that the effects on social attitudes were cumulative is quite staggering when applied to television. The young people in this study saw, at most, only a few films relevant to a given attitude. Although children may pay less attention to TV than to a movie, just think how many shows embodying a single consistent view of social reality are seen by the regular viewer of a TV series. And just think how many different series may present basically similar social attitudes. Thus, the cumulative effects of television are likely to be much larger than those of film.

Research in Sweden speaks to this point. "Television,

over the long term, has given practically all school children impulses to desire a more active, mobile and urban lifestyle. There is, among other things, a greater desire to move, particularly to the towns. Expectations with regard to future occupations have become higher, and partly different in character. Children dream, for example, more often of such glamorous occupations as becoming footballers, pilots, pop singers and film-stars, at the expense of such occupations as those of teacher, craftsman, or shop assistant."[20] A parallel phenomenon was found in England, even when television was at an early stage of development.[21]

CHARACTER RECOGNITION AND IDENTIFICATION

Grant Noble, in *Children in Front of the Small Screen*, suggests that children, through recognizing television characters as similar to people they know, reduce uncertainty about the outcome of the plot and are able to predict what will happen next. Noble contrasts recognition of a character with identification, in which children, losing themselves in the screen, *become* the character. Identification does not lead to skill in predicting what will happen next because, in Noble's words, "Children who have identified with a film hero, who share the here and now of his ongoing film experiences, do not need to look forward in the plot."[22] Although both processes occur in both media, Noble presents evidence that whereas the movies encourage more identification, television tends to encourage more recognition, thereby allowing the child to interact vicariously with a whole social world.

James Hosney has suggested that it may be that children do not lose themselves so much in television because the edges of the TV screen are always at the center of the viewer's visual field. In the movies, the larger screen puts the edges at the periphery of vision, and the lack of distinct edges makes it easier for the viewer to become part of the scene, thus facilitating identification.

The connection between recognition and prediction is supported by Noble's experimental evidence. When a film was stopped in the middle, children who recognized any character in the film as similar to someone they knew were much more likely to predict correctly what the hero or villain would do next. Identification with a character neither helped nor hurt the ability to predict.

Thus, starting with character recognition, children acquire knowledge of predictable behavior patterns within the screen world. Knowledge of such patterns may then be applied off the screen as well as on: children may use similarities between screen characters and real people to make generalizations about the rules and regularities of human behavior.

KNOWLEDGE, FEELING, AND BEHAVIOR

The power of television to change children's social attitudes and their beliefs about the ways people behave in the real world raises the question of how these changes in attitudes affect children's actual behavior. One kind of effect is easy to trace: children often take well-known TV characters as examples to be imitated. The day after Fonzie took out a library card on *Happy Days*, there was a five-fold increase in the number of children applying for library cards in the United States. Details like this, inserted into entertainment programming, could have a very positive effect on children's behavior without requiring any basic change in the nature of TV shows.[23]

The link between television and behavior is a complex

one, influenced by many factors other than the knowledge and attitudes gained from television. However, many research studies have found links between children's viewing of antisocial (such as violent) behavior on television and their own subsequent behavior, and another body of evidence indicates that seeing positive social behavior, such as helping and cooperation, on television can influence children to act in more prosocial ways. As with social *knowledge*, television as a model for *behavior* can work in opposite directions, depending on the content of the program.[24]

The long-term effects of television on behavior are harder to determine than its long-term effects on knowledge and attitudes. But knowledge and attitudes often do influence action. For example, a child's attitude toward and knowledge about a minority group will obviously affect how the child acts upon meeting a member of that group.

Sometimes feelings are the connecting link among television, knowledge, and behavior. An example is the use of television to reduce children's fear of undergoing surgery. Children between the ages of four and twelve who were about to have various types of surgery were shown video films of a child being hospitalized and undergoing surgery. Compared to a similar group who had seen an unrelated film, these children were less fearful, both before and after their operations, and showed less postoperative problem behavior.[25]

This use of television in a hospital makes an important point: in thinking about the relationship between children and television, we should not limit ourselves to broadcast television. Advances in video technology have created immense possibilities for special-purpose films for specific audiences. Already there is a body of scientific literature on the therapeutic use of film to diminish anxiety.

Television (or film) is better suited to this kind of emotional education than is print.[26] For example, a pamphlet might have been used to prepare the children for surgery, but no matter how clever the presentation, it would have been at a disadvantage. Print is linear and sequential; it can present only one thing at a time. But emotional reactions generally occur simultaneously with other events. Partly because language is sequential and partly because each individual word carries only a portion of a complete thought, it takes relatively great effort to convey a piece of information in print. This is one reason "a picture is worth a thousand words." (While television is better at presenting a character's visible feelings, print is better at presenting inner thoughts; this point will be discussed in Chapter 6.)

For the presurgery film to succeed, it had to show the surgery patient's feelings about what was happening, not just present information about events. The power of television to stimulate memorable emotions is demonstrated by a study of Swiss teenagers, in which emotional reactions to television characters persisted for three weeks, while strictly cognitive effects of the show diminished in this same time period.[27]

Print also cannot present the events of the surgery as realistically as can television or film. The realism of film makes it much easier for the viewer (in this case the patient) to recognize what is happening to him or her as similar to the film and therefore makes it easier to apply the learning from the film to the real situation.

This power of television and film to communicate feeling can be a danger as well as a benefit. The stimulation of an emotion in a situation, like television, where it has no real-world consequences can result in a desensitizing of feeling. For example, researchers have found that televised violence makes children more tolerant of aggression in other children and less emotionally responsive to violence themselves. In the words of an eleven-year-old interviewed by *Newsweek*: "You see so much violence that it's meaningless. If I saw someone really get killed, it wouldn't be a big deal. I guess I'm turning into a hard rock."[28]

The arousal of emotion through showing adult situations that children would not otherwise generally be exposed to can have other effects as well. In England in the late 1950s, adolescents with televisions were more worried about growing up than similar adolescents who did not have television sets.[29] It is as though day-after-day exposure to the adult world as portrayed on television makes young people more fearful about creating their own adult world.

LEARNING TO BE A CONSUMER

An important part of children's social reality is their role as consumers. Television has an obvious impact on children as consumers in countries like the United States, where television is an almost purely commercial venture and television advertising is an important part of children's exposure to the medium. However, television also affects the child as consumer even when there is no advertising at all. In the 1950s it was found that British children who had access only to the BBC, which carries no advertising, had more materialistic ambitions than those without television. Adolescent boys who watched television, for example, were more focused on what they would *have* in the future; adolescent boys without television were more focused on what they would be *doing*. The longer the child's experience with television, the more this materialistic outlook increased.[30] Apparently, the visual images of television create an emphasis on visible and tangible objects, hence on consumption, in defining one's identity and life style.

Formal features of television also influence the child's development as a consumer. Commercials in the United States are heavily visual, action-oriented, quick-paced, and repetitive, and use catchy music and jingles. All of these are features that catch attention and promote learning even among quite young children, as the research on *Sesame Street* showed. (Indeed, the creators of *Sesame Street* got some of their ideas from studying the techniques used in commercials.)

Parents in the United States tend to fear the teaching potential of commercials. Because advertisers have perfected their teaching techniques, this fear is justified. Children do attend to and learn from commercials. They remember slogans, jingles, and brand names. They often try to influence their parents to buy advertised goods. Children below age seven or so are particularly vulnerable to such effects, probably because they do not discriminate between the program and the commercial and do not realize that the purpose of commercials is to sell goods;[31] they simply accept commercials as presenting information like any other television format.

What can be done? It turns out that the impact of commercials can be very much affected by discussion and instruction. For example, researchers at UCLA developed curricula for the second and fourth grades to help children understand the purpose and nature of commercials, so that they would make more effective consumer decisions. The curriculum that worked best explained how commercials create needs and desires in children. It also stressed paying attention to the information in the commercial, and it stimulated children to be more reflective and ask questions about commercials. One week after the three half-hour lessons, children in both grades found advertised products less desirable, understood commercials better, and found them less credible.[32]

The success of this brief educational program shows that it is not very difficult to counteract television's power to teach when such teaching is not in the children's best interests. This curriculum was developed for school use, but parents can use the same techniques at home: point out that commercials are designed to sell by creating needs; question the methods used (such as exaggeration); and generally make commercials a subject for discussion, evaluation, and questioning.

TELEVISION AS REALITY

One reason children are so vulnerable to the messages of television is that they take what they see on television to be reality. Very young children equate all of television except cartoons with reality. Aimée Dorr tells an anecdote about her three-year-old son, who saw her being interviewed on television: "His father reported that he called out my name, asked me questions, and tried to show me things. He became quite angry when I continued to ignore his attempts to engage me in social interchange and finally left the room in disgust."[33] Much research shows that this confusion of television with reality diminishes steadily with age.

As children get older they adopt new definitions of television reality: first they believe that anything on television that *could* happen in the real world is real on television; later they believe that what they see on television represents something that *probably* happens in the real world. But despite these changes in the meaning of reality, the belief that entertainment programming represents social reality does not seem to change much with greater life experience or exposure to television. The realistic style of much entertainment programming seems to contribute to this effect.[34]

Furthermore, if children either recognize characters

on television as being like someone they know or identify with them, this greater personal involvement leads
them to consider the program more real. Since children
tend to identify with the fantastic characters on television (such as Superman) and to recognize the realistic ones, powerful factors operate to get the child to
treat the televised world as real.[35] This belief in the reality of the televised world makes children of all age groups
vulnerable to the social messages of television.

Children recognize books as fiction sooner than television.[36] Apparently, the fact that print does not physically resemble the things and events it symbolizes makes
it easier to separate its content from the real world. Thus,
as many have feared, television, with its presentation
of live action, is a more seductive medium in transforming fantasy into reality. But what is a negative effect in
the presentation of fiction can be a positive one in the
presentation of fact. Television can be an extremely compelling medium for teaching children about the real world.
In Scandinavia it was found that if eleven-year-olds learn
of the same news event from television, parents, teachers, and the newspaper, the majority will rely primarily
on television. They consider television the best-in-
formed medium, and they say that on television "you
can see for yourself what is happening."[37]

Minority children and children of low socioeconomic
status are typically the most vulnerable to having their
concepts of social reality shaped by television, for, in
the United States, they are even more likely than white
and middle-class children to believe in the realism of
the world presented on the screen.[38] This may be merely
an example of the principle that the less you know about
an area the more power television has to define that
area for you. The world of U.S. television is predomi-
nantly white and middle-class, and thus it is, on the
average, more familiar to white and middle-class chil-

dren than to those from minority groups and those of lower socioeconomic status. According to this principle, a minority or working-class child with extensive personal experience within the middle-class white world would, like middle-class white children, be less vulnerable to the television view of this world.

While television has more power to define the unknown, the unknown is also more likely to be misunderstood. For example, a program about a middle-class family is understood better by young middle-class children than by working-class children, and a program about a working-class family is understood better by young working-class children.[39] Thus, portrayals of a social milieu unlike the child's own will be less understood, even while they have greater power to shape the child's view of that milieu.

A child's attitudes and beliefs can function as a defense against television messages that contradict them. Children with stereotyped views of sex roles remember a still picture better if it agrees with their views than if it contradicts them.[40] Thus attitudes are a defense against nonstereotyped images. Social beliefs can lead not only to selective memory, but also to boomerang effects on attitudes. In an experiment in the United States, nonsexist commercials were shown to children aged eight, ten, and thirteen. After seeing the commercials, the eight- and ten-year-olds, both boys and girls, endorsed less traditional roles for women. But there was a boomerang effect among the thirteen-year-old boys, who gave an even stronger endorsement of traditional roles for women. Just entering a period of working out their own masculine identities, these boys may have found the message of the commercials threatening. (The age differences also reflect the general finding that younger viewers are more open to messages from the media than are older ones.) A similar boomerang effect was found in England among adolescents who watched a program presenting men and women in nontraditional occupational roles. Such reactions against television's messages occur when those messages clash with a child's pre-existing attitudes. They demonstrate that the effects of television are a function of what the child brings to the medium, not only of what the medium brings to the child.[41]

WHAT PARENTS CAN DO

Almost no research has been done on what parents would probably most like to know: how to counteract the influence of the social information children get from television. We do know that by discussing shows with children, parents or other adults can increase the benefits and decrease the negative effects of watching commercial television programs.[42] For example, adult interpretation of *Batman* made elementary-school children more critical of the violence in the show, and, as mentioned earlier, adult interpretation of an episode of *All in the Family* led children to be more accepting of nontraditional sex roles.

To be more specific, parents can affect what social knowledge children take away from a show by highlighting important information and by interpreting what is going on in the show. In a study of this type of situation, four- and five-year-olds watched an episode of the family-hour program *Adam-12*. The episode dealt with students being truant from school and getting into trouble. One group of students watched the show with a teacher who made neutral comments such as "Let's sit here and watch a TV show." A second group watched with the same teacher, but the teacher made explanatory comments such as "Oh, no! That boy is in trouble. He did not go to school when he was supposed to. He was playing hookey and that is bad." Children in the second group learned more specific details of the program, increased their knowledge of truancy, and increased their positive attitudes in the direction of the teacher's comments. The differences between the two groups were still evident one week later, indicating that the discussion promoted retention as well as immediate learning.[43]

This simple process is one that parents can easily follow at home, if they are willing to watch television with their children. Observation of what actually goes on in homes indicates that parents and children often do watch television together, but that the parents seldom provide this type of commentary.[44]

Although television in the United States may sometimes seem to put forth a uniform message about the nature of the social world, we have seen that diverse messages do exist and that television can have quite opposite influences on social attitudes depending on program content. These facts have an obvious yet important implication for parents: select shows for your children and help the children to be selective themselves. While all parents will not agree on the social values they want to teach their children, all parents do socialize their children into one set of values or another. Selection, as well as discussion of television programs, needs to be looked upon not as a form of censorship but as an extension of this normal and universal process of socialization.

It is useful to remember that television seems to be especially influential in forming attitudes and knowledge on topics with which the child lacks experience. Children who have first-hand knowledge of a topic make a clearer separation between the real world and the television world.[45] Thus, parents can counteract television by giving their children first-hand experience in areas

they consider important. For example, a way to counteract the ethnic stereotypes on television is to expose
your child to people from different ethnic groups.

WHAT SCHOOLS CAN DO

Aimée Dorr and her colleagues have developed two
courses in critical television skills to encourage young
children to question the reality of what they see on television. Each curriculum combines taped program segments, group discussion, role playing, games, and
commentary by the teacher. The "industry curriculum"
emphasizes the lack of realism in entertainment programming and the industry's economic system; for example, the fact that programs are broadcast to make
money. The "process curriculum" is designed to teach
children processes and sources for judging television
realism; it emphasizes that programs vary in realism.

In a test of these courses, the industry curriculum
produced the most skepticism about the reality of a television show. (The show was *The Jeffersons*, a situation
comedy that presents a rather stereotypical view of a
black family.) The process curriculum led to more balanced judgments in which children decided that the
show was both real and pretend. Perhaps most important, these two curricula developed in children a questioning attitude toward the social reality portrayed on
television.[46]

This work shows that children as young as age five
can be taught, in a relatively short time, to make critical
judgments about the reality of what they see on television. Such school programs can help transform child
viewers from passive consumers to active critics of the
social world presented on entertainment television.

5 / Using Television to Overcome Educational Disadvantage

Television is, in certain respects, an intrinsically democratic medium. Within the United States and other developed countries, it is democratic in that it reduces the advantage possessed by middle-class people in the world of schools and books. On a global scale, it is democratic because it can help alleviate the problems of educational development in the Third World. If knowledge is power, television, because of its psychological and material accessibility, has the potential to help redistribute this power more widely in society and among societies, particularly through its use in the educational system. (This potential is rather independent of the fact that, in other respects, notably the control of the medium, television is elitist rather than democratic.)[1] This potential to spread education grows out of the way the medium can, at its best, be made to fit both the nature of its subject matter and the minds of its audience.

With Jessica Beagles-Roos, I did some research involving children aged six to ten from four different groups: middle-class white, middle-class black, working-class white, and working-class black. Each child watched an animated, narrated story on a TV monitor; at a different time, the child heard another story played on a cassette player/radio. Right after seeing or hearing each story, the child was tested for comprehension and memory.

The results can throw light on the role of television in education, because the radio presentation is similar to what happens in the classroom: the child hears the teacher lecture or have exchanges with other children. Like a radio presentation, the classroom stimulus is basically a verbal one. The television presentation adds dynamic visual illustration.

Television led to more overall learning of the stories than did radio, whether learning was measured by verbal or visual knowledge. Some of our learning measures showed no class or ethnic differences; a few did, with differences favoring the groups that generally do better in school-related tasks of all kinds. That is, middle-class children of both ethnic groups learned better from television than working-class children; white children of both classes learned better from radio than black. But the class and ethnic differences were far smaller than the differences between the two media. The average working-class child learned much more from a television presentation than the average middle-class child did from a radio presentation, and the average black child learned more from a television presentation than the average white child did from a radio presentation.

The medium of television did not erase class or ethnic differences. But to the extent that, in education, we are interested in skill levels rather than group comparisons (and I firmly believe that skill level is what counts), these results have important implications. They suggest that television can raise the level of learning in all groups to above what it is in *any* group without the medium.

SESAME STREET AND THE DISADVANTAGED

Over the years, there has been debate about whether *Sesame Street* closes the gap between disadvantaged and advantaged preschool children. The conclusion is that it does not close this gap, either in the United States or in Israel. This is understandable: we cannot expect a TV show to eliminate a knowledge gap created by many forces in society. However, what is important about *Sesame Street* in the United States (and in Australia and Israel as well) is that disadvantaged groups do learn what is taught on the show, and that they learn more if they watch more. They also learn best the skills that receive the most time and attention on the show. In other words, learning is proportional to exposure to *Sesame Street*.[2]

There is a lot more equality between children of different ethnic and socioeconomic groups in their response to *Sesame Street* than in their response to schools. In the United States in 1973, more than 90 percent of inner-city preschool children were watching *Sesame Street* in cities where it was broadcast on a commercial channel.[3] Thus, the program was not viewed more by middle-class children than by poor, urban children. Disadvantaged groups have, in contrast, relatively high dropout and truancy rates from school. As a group of *Sesame Street* researchers put it, "Although the classroom may be an uncomfortable place for many children, particularly those who have not come from middle-class homes, television is part of the child's own turf."[4]

The point here is not, of course, that children from the disadvantaged groups in a society have a lesser ability to learn from print or other media in school. Rather, it is that they have fewer opportunities in their backgrounds for experience with books and with school-like situations and so they are at a disadvantage in classrooms oriented toward reading and lectures. In contrast, their backgrounds, at least in industrialized countries like the United States and Britain, may provide an advantage in learning from television because of greater exposure and more favorable attitudes at home toward the medium.

THE ELECTRIC COMPANY: TEACHING READING

The Electric Company is an example of how television can reach children who have not succeeded in school. It accomplishes this goal by systematically using features that are unique to television. The show was created in 1971 by the Children's Television Workshop as an experiment in using television to teach reading skills to second-, third-, and fourth-grade children who were having difficulty in learning to read in school. Like *Sesame Street*, the show attracted a large audience: at one point, the audience was estimated at about eleven million and the program was used in 35 percent of all elementary schools in the United States. Watching *The Electric Company* improved a wide variety of reading skills. It was particularly effective with beginning readers (first graders) and with second graders who scored in the lower half of their grade on standard reading tests. All groups, black and white, Spanish-speaking and English-speaking, benefited equally from the program. Thus, *The Electric Company* demonstrates the egalitarian nature of television and its ability to provide educational help selectively to those most in need.[5]

Many features undoubtedly contribute to the success of *The Electric Company*: the medium of television is second nature to its audience; the show presents children from many cultural backgrounds; it is set in an urban street scene familiar to many disadvantaged children; it uses rock music; it has humor. In addition, the show uses forms unique to television (or film) to present concretely and directly difficult reading concepts that a teacher using print can present only abstractly and indirectly.

One of the most difficult tasks in beginning reading is blending the sounds of individual letters into larger units such as complete words. *The Electric Company* has successfully taught this skill.[6] Through the use of visual movement and synchronized voice, the show has graphically modeled the blending process. In one such segment, two featureless profiles are face to face a short distance apart on the screen. (Profiles are used because research showed that facial features distract children's attention away from letters.) The character on the left pronounces, with slightly exaggerated lip movements, the first element of a word, for example "ch." As it is pronounced, the letters *ch* appear to emerge from the character's mouth and move to the lower middle of the screen. (Exaggerated lip movement is used because it attracts visual attention to the place where the print will emerge.) The routine is then repeated, with the last half of the word, perhaps "ip," emerging from the mouth of the character on the right. Finally, the two print elements slide together to form a single unit, "chip," as that unit is pronounced by the two actors in unison. In teaching blends it is important to make clear what letters are being pronounced when. Television can do this easily. Making letters brighter, expanding them, wiggling them, or making them jump, just at the moment when they are being pronounced, makes it likely that the child will associate the right sound with the right letter in the blend.[7]

These techniques have two important characteristics. First, the dynamic visual quality of television models an "invisible" aspect of reading, blending, that is difficult to describe or to illustrate with static materials. Thus, the dynamic visual forms of television fit the mental operations that constitute the process of reading. I believe that this fit is a key part of what makes television a good teaching tool.

The second characteristic is the use of movement to direct attention. For example, the moving lips bring children's attention to the mouth. In directing the child's visual attention, the show puts into practice the principle that attention is a prerequisite for comprehension and learning.[8] Thus, the techniques used in *The Electric Company* involve a careful match between the desired mental processes and the forms used to elicit them. One reason why *The Electric Company* succeeds where schools fail is that the forms of television can create a much closer match to the mental processes of beginning reading than conventional methods ever could.

TELEVISION, INTERACTION WITH AN ADULT, AND THE KNOWLEDGE GAP

A pervasive finding in television research is that the effects of television programs on knowledge are stronger if an adult interacts with the child during the viewing process. The adult can encourage the child to pay attention, can make interpretations, and can explain things the child finds incomprehensible. Watching with the child is not enough; it is crucial to talk about the show being watched.[9] In fact, research on *Sesame Street* in both the United States and Israel indicates that, to a great extent, the gap in learning between disadvantaged and advantaged children closes if the disadvantaged children have an adult to watch and discuss the programs with them[10]

While this type of discussion with an adult can happen at home, an adult is not always available. At school, in contrast, the teacher is always available for this role. This suggests that bringing high-quality, attractive educational television into the classroom and integrating it into classroom discussion might significantly reduce the educational gaps between advantaged and disadvantaged children.

TELEVISION AND EDUCATION IN NIGER

Some Third World countries have used television to bring education to children whose parents lacked either formal education or literacy. These experiences demonstrate that television can be effective as the primary means of education in situations where not just certain groups, but the overwhelming majority of the population is "educationally disadvantaged" from the point of view of formal education.

The most dramatic example is Téléniger in the country of Niger, which started in 1964. Through television, Téléniger brought the first five grades to children who not only were "educationally disadvantaged" but did not even speak the language of the school, which was French. Another disadvantage was the absence of trained teachers.[11]

Téléniger avoided the trap of making the form of an earlier medium the content of the newer one: it did not use television to present teachers giving televised lectures. Instead, the project broke new ground in trying to use all the techniques special to the medium of television. For example, much was taught through dramatic skits, often set in traditional villages similar to the children's own.

In the area of language teaching, Téléniger took advantage of television's ability to present not only "talk" but also the visible context that made the talk meaningful. For example, an object would be presented on the screen and then named. Later, the image would be removed, and the child would be asked to remember the meaning of the word. This method contrasts with the more usual language instruction in which what is being talked about is not present and must be evoked by translation—a relatively ineffective method of teaching a second language.

Téléniger also designed formats so as to encourage participation. A motto was "Children are more *actors* than spectators."

Teaching French was central to education in Niger because it was both a foreign language (the language of Niger's colonizers) and the language of instruction. Therefore, the results in the study of French were particularly important. Anecdotally, it is reported that French visitors to Niger were surprised at how well the children were speaking after only two or three years. The children scored well on standardized tests in all subjects (all given in French). In addition, there was an absence of being held back to repeat a grade level, generally a rather pervasive feature of the French educational system, even in France; pupils became very attached to the school, even coming when the teacher was absent; and the time necessary to pass the test for the standardized elementary school certificate was reduced from six to five years. And all of this was done without trained teachers, using people who had only an elementary education themselves plus three months of special training for the project.

The teachers' job was not primarily to lecture (which they could not have done, probably, without more training), but to help the children understand the TV screen and to encourage the children to talk about the program. The children were also encouraged to respond even more actively, for example by acting out skits based on what they had seen in the show. This is particularly interesting in light of the fact that research has indicated (for example in Colombia) that the combination of television with a more involving student activity like discussion is more effective for learning than television plus lecture. Thus, the absence of trained teachers may actually have been an advantage to the project because it required more active student participation in the learning process. The importance of active participation by students comes up again and again in the results of research into the educational use of media.

The example of Téléniger shows the immense potential of television for overcoming educational disadvantage. Clearly this potential applies to educational development in the Third World, as well as to children from less advantaged groups within the industrialized countries.

CULTURAL COMPATIBILITY

While television's appeal and ability to communicate may be universal, the style and content of programming need to be adapted to individual cultures. Sometimes a program format that is successful in one culture will not work in another. This happened when a Spanish version of *Sesame Street* was tried out in Mexico. About half of each program was locally produced, with characters, settings, and speech indigenous to Central and South America, if not specifically to Mexico. When the show was tested in Mexico City, children from very poor families learned from it, as they did in the United States.[12] But when the show was tested in rural areas, it failed to achieve its learning goals. As Hilde Himmelweit puts it, "The rapid change of scenes and characters, designed to hold the attention of American city children, proved distracting to Mexican children used to a slower, less jerky rhythm of life."[13]

The universality of the medium should not be an excuse for a new form of cultural imperialism in which the television "haves" indiscriminately distribute their programming around the world. The television "have nots" need also to consider the cultural suitability of programs that are for sale to their countries.

An important feature of television is its broad accessibility. Children develop basic television literacy by simply watching television; no one needs to be taught to "read" television's symbolic code. In addition, the hardware of television is inexpensive enough to be available on a mass scale. Evidence from different subcultures and countries shows that children who are at an educational disadvantage in the world of lectures and books do not have this same disadvantage when it comes to learning from television. Properly used, the medium of television could do much to raise both the minimum and the average levels of education in the industrialized countries and the Third World alike.

Up to now, I have not mentioned the artistic quality and production values of television programs. In addition to good educational design, a program's aesthetic and creative qualities are undoubtedly important to its educational success. An attempt at educational reform using television in El Salvador had variable results depending mainly on the quality of particular programs.[14] Although it is difficult to measure such intangibles as artistic quality, it is important to keep in mind that television is an art as well as a technology. The full exploitation of television's educational potential must depend on using the art, as well as on knowing the technology, the child, the culture, and the subject matter.

6 / Comparing Print, Radio, and Television

"The medium is the message." McLuhan meant that each medium has effects on the way people's minds work, effects that are independent of the content being transmitted by the medium. We have seen in earlier chapters that watching television, for example, does indeed seem to give today's children certain mental skills that those of us raised before the widespread availability of television do not have. (Chapters 7 and 8 will show how the mental abilities developed by watching television may help children master the newer media of video games and other computer technology.)

Those who worry about the effects of television on children's minds compare television, implicitly or explicitly, with print. Kids can't read anymore, they say, and it's all the fault of television. Our educational system is built around print and reading. There is a common assumption that print is the intellectually superior medium—that television, by comparison, encourages children to be passive, mindless, and unimaginative.

Historically, the medium that followed print was not television but radio. Today in the United States, radio is quite specialized for music; very little children's programming exists on radio, and few children listen to it. But for the pre-TV generation, radio was an influential medium. If we want to know what psychological changes television has caused, it is useful to compare it not only with print but also with its immediate historical predecessor, radio.

It may be that print, radio, and television foster different psychological and social processes in their audiences. To investigate this possibility, I shall consider what each medium added, psychologically, to the one that came before it. This investigation should yield some insight into the distinctive contribution each medium can make to human development.

PRINT AND INTELLECTUAL PROCESSES

Print was the first technology of mass communication. It was not, however, the first symbolic medium of human communication. Oral language and face-to-face communication long preceded it. So the first question to ask about print is what it adds to face-to-face communication in terms of impact on human development.

An obvious feature of print is that it permits the accumulation of knowledge by creating a way to store information. Hence, the coming of print gave any literate individual access to a vastly larger store of knowledge than was possible in a nonliterate culture. Another claim, more interesting from the point of view of the changes in consciousness brought about by different media, is that learning to read and write affects the processes of thinking, the ways people classify, reason, and remember.

In most cultures, the ability to read and write is inextricably tied up with schooling, so that it is impossible to separate the effects of literacy in itself from those of formal education. But in Liberia there is a cultural group, the Vai, who maintain a writing system outside the context of schooling. Two ingenious researchers, Sylvia

Scribner and Michael Cole, studied the Vai to examine the psychological effects of literacy apart from those of formal education.[1]

Within the Vai culture are to be found three different literacies, each with its own particular set of learning conditions and patterns of use: Vai writing, acquired by adults through informal means; Arabic, learned by children in the Koranic school; and English writing, taught in European-style schools. Thus the Vai people provide an opportunity to assess the psychological consequences of different conditions of literacy learning and use. The Vai also provide a control group, the majority of the population, who have not had the opportunity to acquire any form of literacy.

Scribner and Cole's most important finding was a negative one: they discovered very little effect of print literacy in general. Instead, the different literacies, each with its own methods of learning and use, had different effects.

Verbal explanation and schooling. School-based English literacy, for example, led to the development of a general skill in verbal explanation. Since Arabic and Vai literacy did not have this effect, it must not be the ability to read and write, in itself, that fosters explanatory skills; the development of skill in verbal explanation must be produced by other aspects of schooling. Scribner and Cole ascribe special importance to teacher-pupil dialogue in the classroom: teachers ask questions that give students practice in formulating explanations, questions like "What made you give that answer?"

The finding that it is formal education, not literacy in itself, that fosters the most widely generalized intellectual skills has great educational significance. It indicates that print may not be a superior medium for education: that what goes on between teacher and student may be more central to the effects of schooling than is the medium of instruction. In Chapter 5 we saw that discussion with an adult is an important key to what children learn from a television program. Thus, in the right context of dialogue and discussion, television can take the role traditionally reserved for print, while without this context print loses its power as an educational medium. I shall come back to this important theme in later chapters, particularly Chapter 9, where I suggest greater use of the electronic media in schools.

Letter writing and verbal explicitness. The Vai use both English and Vai, but not Arabic, to write letters. (Arabic is used primarily for rote learning of the Koran.) In an experiment, people were asked to dictate a letter giving directions on how to play a new board game or how to get to their farm. The notion was more information must be made verbally explicit in a letter than in face-to-face communication, where gesture and other nonverbal means can carry part of a message. For example, in explaining a board game, pieces can be identified by pointing in face-to-face communication, but they must be verbally described in a letter. This analysis was borne out by the results. Both those literate in Vai and those literate in English provided more explicit verbal information in their dictated letters than illiterates did, but there was no difference between the illiterates and those literate in Arabic. Once again, it was not the nature of the medium itself—print—that was responsible for this effect but its *use*: the fact that Vai people use written Vai and written English to communicate at a distance with people through letters.

Writing and the spoken language. It is an established generalization that written language tends to be more historically conservative than spoken language. Old forms that have disappeared from speaking will be maintained in writing. An interesting question follows: Is a literate person's speech influenced by exposure to written language, with its more archaic forms? Steven Reder, a linguist working with Scribner and Cole, identified a particular sound ("l" in the middle of a word) that was disappearing from spoken Vai. He then compared the speech of literates and illiterates with respect to this sound, and found that literates did tend to use the sound more than illiterates. Although the frequency of a particular sound may not be a very earth-shattering effect of literacy, the principle is an important one: one medium of communication (in this case, writing) can alter a person's style of communication in another medium (in this case, speaking).

Reder's findings can be applied to the mass media. Radio and television, being modes of oral rather than written communication, are not likely to have the conservative influence on speech that writing has. Hence, spoken language may now, under their influence, be changing more rapidly than when print was the main medium of mass communication. This rapid change may be one factor behind the widespread impression that our language is deteriorating at an ever accelerating pace and that children speak less well than their elders. Language change is interpreted as deterioration from the standard created in an earlier era. The more rapid the change, the more serious the perceived deterioration. Viewed historically, however, today's error may be tomorrow's standard form.

LITERACY AND SOCIAL INTERACTION

Mallory Wober examined the social consequences of literacy in a study in Nigeria. Two very different types of housing were available to workers in a company. One type was housing in a typical urban African setting: the population was dense, much life went on in the street, it was noisy, and there was music blaring everywhere.

The other type was European-style housing in a suburban housing development provided by the company: houses were separated by yards in a quiet residential neighborhood; there was good plumbing for bathrooms and kitchens. Wober found that one reason given for choosing the second type of housing was to be alone in peace and quiet to read.[2] Thus, print literacy seemed to be one factor leading them to reject an environment characterized by a high degree of social contact.

If Wober's finding captures a general truth about literacy, then literacy is the original medium of social isolation. McLuhan realized this twenty years ago; as he put it, "We are no more prepared to encounter radio and TV in our literate milieu than the native of Ghana is able to cope with the literacy that takes him out of his collective tribal world and beaches him in individual isolation."[3] Literacy was the first medium of communication that required solitude for its effective practice.

This is an important point to remember when we hear complaints about the isolating effects of television, video games, or computers. Without reducing the problem, it does place it in historical perspective. (Indeed, the accumulated research concerning the effect of television on children's patterns of social interaction indicates that television has absolutely no effect on the amount of time children spend in various sorts of social engagement.)[4]

COMPARING PRINT, RADIO, AND TELEVISION

The evidence here is of a very different sort from Cole and Scribner's work on literacy. Kathy Pezdek and Ariella Lehrer conducted an investigation of whether the same cognitive processes are required to extract information and meaning from radio and television as to understand print. A group of second graders and sixth graders read one story aloud from a picture book and heard another story in a radio presentation; another group read aloud one story and watched the other in a television presentation. Following each story, the children were given various tests of comprehension and memory.

There was a positive correlation between reading scores and listening scores on both comprehension and memory tests. That is, a child who read aloud with good comprehension and memory for the material was also likely to comprehend and remember material heard on the radio. These results indicate that there is an overlap between the information-processing skills called up by print and radio. The probable reason for this overlap is that both are exclusively verbal media.

In contrast to the findings for print and radio, there was not a significant positive correlation between reading scores and "watching" scores on any of the tests. That is, a child who watched a story with good comprehension or memory was not necessarily a child who showed equal skill in reading the story; skills in extracting and remembering information from the two media showed themselves to be relatively independent of each other.

Very recently, however, Miri Ben-Moshe and Gavriel Salomon have found that training sixth graders to watch television in a more active, careful way by asking penetrating questions about the shows improves their reading comprehension scores.[6] This indicates that, under particular conditions, there can be an overlap between reading skills and viewing skills. It seems that whether or not the two media stimulate the same processes depends on *how the medium is being used*. There is evidence that television does interfere with reading under some circumstances,[7] but this may happen not because of an intrinsic conflict between these two media but because the usual way of watching television is without care or effort.[8] I shall return to this point later.

Comparing the levels of comprehension and memory in print and in television, Pezdek and Lehrer found only one statistically reliable difference between print and television, and it favored television. Thus, in terms of learning, print does not seem to deserve its exalted reputation, television its negative one.

Pezdek and Lehrer also found that television led to better comprehension and memory than radio did. This result (which has also been found by Jessica Beagles-Roos and myself and by other researchers)[9] is particularly interesting because a number of the tests were verbal. It indicates that the addition of dynamic visual images makes verbally presented information easier to remember. Thus, television is a more effective medium than radio for transmitting information to children.

These experiments confirm the special power television has for learning. Children tend to learn what they see on television more thoroughly than what they read or hear on radio or tape. This power means that the responsibility of television producers is much greater, the need for quality more pressing than with the older media.

DIFFERENCES IN VERBAL STYLE

In terms of verbal style, radio resembles print, while television resembles face-to-face oral communication. This fits with the point that reading and listening involve some of the same information-processing skills, while television, under usual viewing circumstances, involves a different set of skills.

Vague reference. My colleagues and I did a study comparing radio and television.[10] We had each child hear or see a program, then asked the child to retell the story to an adult who, the child was told, was unfamiliar with it. An interesting stylistic difference in response to the two media emerged: the children made more vague references to characters in retelling the television stories than in retelling the radio stories.

An example of a vague reference is the use of a pronoun, such as "he" or "she" without an antecedent noun. Another example is the use of a general term like "the boy" or "the woman" without earlier identification. Pronouns or general terms of reference are normally used when the identity of a referent has already been established either verbally, for example with a proper name, or nonverbally, for example by pointing or looking at the referent in question. Under these circumstances, the referent becomes "old" information and the use of a pronoun or general term is not vague.

I believe that the vague character references that occur in the retelling of television stories are probably not vague to the teller. What I think is happening is that the teller has the visual image of the character in mind, from having seen it on television, and therefore refers to it as old information, by means of a pronoun or general term. The problem, of course, is that the listener cannot see the image the speaker has in mind. Therefore, from the listener's point of view, the use of a pronoun or general term under these circumstances is vague and does not communicate enough information.

When retelling stories they have heard on radio or tape, children have no such visual mental image, and therefore their narratives contain more verbally explicit information. This quality of radio parallels the effect of literacy on the Vai's dictated letters. Indeed, radio as a medium is structurally similar to writing: in both, the message must be verbally self-contained and therefore explicit. Neither writing nor radio can expand or explicate a message through visual communication. In this important respect, these media differ from face-to-face communication and television.

I cannot prove the connection to television, but as a teacher I have noticed an inordinate amount of vague reference in university students' writing. It occurs to me that this could be a long-term effect of large quantities of television watching. In other words, the immediate effect of television, seen in our study, repeated many, many times, could turn into a general approach to communication. Such an approach may be adequate in face-to-face interaction, where both participants can often see what they are talking about, but it is not adequate in writing, where nonverbal cues are lacking.

Vague reference on television. One reason why television viewers, children or adults, may use vague reference is that vague reference is common in the verbal communication presented on television. I used baseball broadcasts as a controlled experiment to test this. Because the same games are often broadcast on both radio and television, I could tape the narration of the same moments of play of the same game in both media. I taped several innings from the fourth game of the 1982 World Series between the St. Louis Cardinals and the Milwaukee Brewers. Comparison of samples from the transcripts of the two different media gives preliminary support to my analysis.

As anticipated, there was more vague reference in the television version than in the radio version of the game. I looked at how the batters were described at the decisive moment when they either hit, struck out, or walked. In about half the instances, the identity of the batter was taken for granted in the television account, but not in the radio account. The television announcer apparently relied on the visual image to identify the batter, while the radio announcer mentioned his name. Vague reference extended to action as well. Occasionally the television announcer would name the batter, relying on the visual image to say what the batter had done, while the radio announcer would both name the batter and describe his action. These preliminary results indicate that television presents a verbal model that, when it is inappropriately transferred to writing, is labeled as vague reference.

Two styles of communication. If this analysis is correct, vague reference derives from an audiovisual style of communication in which a visual image carries part of the message, words the other part. It contrasts with a purely verbal style in which words carry the entire message. Analysis of the baseball transcripts suggests other ways in which television narrative has its own distinctive audiovisual style, while radio has a verbal style. For example, more orienting information (such as the score) was given in the radio broadcast than in the television one. This parallels Scribner and Cole's finding that Vai who were literate in Vai or English provided more orienting information in their verbal instructions than the nonliterates did.

This analysis of the stylistic differences between radio and television suggests that children exposed to a particular electronic medium are being exposed to a very particular model of verbal style. I observed earlier that television promotes children's use of vague reference. It now appears that vague reference is one element in a more general audiovisual style of communication. Television also promotes other aspects of an audiovisual style in children's face-to-face communication.

Evidence on this point comes from some research by Laurene Meringoff, who observed that children more often used gesture in retelling a story they had seen on television than in retelling one that had been read to them from a picture book.[11] Very often, these gestures constituted a nonverbal way of talking about some action that had occurred in the film. Thus, because of its dynamic depiction of action, television led to a greater integration of visual with verbal communication than did the storybook presentation.

In sum, radio is like print in that it presents and therefore fosters an articulate verbal style of communication. Television is like face-to-face communication in that it presents and therefore fosters an audiovisual style. Historically, with the advent of print, there was a movement away from the audiovisual style. Radio represented continuity in that it reinforced this change. Television, however, brings a movement back to the audiovisual style. I believe that television is, for this reason, perceived as a threat to the historical and cultural progression which preceded it. I think, too, that this change in style of communication is an important reason for the feeling that television is not only a threat to print culture, but is ruining the spoken language as well.

MEDIA AND OUR SENSES

Do the media affect the relative importance of our senses? Does a visual medium like television, for example, teach its audience to rely on visual information more than on aural information? Writing of what he called "the ratio among our senses," Marshall McLuhan raised this question years ago in *The Gutenberg Galaxy*, where he considered the effects of literacy, and in *Understanding Media*, where he discussed the electronic media. McLuhan had no hard scientific evidence with which to answer the question, and he gave little thought to the question as it concerned children. But in the past five years a body of evidence has accumulated that applies this question to children and their development.

We know that when children watch television, they derive more information from the visual than from the audio track.[12] However, one wonders if children simply have difficulty understanding and remembering verbal material or if the moving visuals distract them from it. For five-year-olds, television does not seem to reduce attention to audio information; overall, at this age the audio is equally comprehensible and memorable whether it is part of a television presentation or presented as a separate soundtrack.[13] It seems that young children simply have a harder time remembering verbal material than visual material.

The story is different for older children. Beagles-Roos and I found that as children advance in age they become better able to recall purely verbal information. With older children, furthermore, the impact of purely verbal information is greater in radio than television presentation.[14] In comparing recall of television and radio stories, we found more dialogue was quoted in retelling the radio versions, even though the same dialogue had been presented on both soundtracks.[14] Thus, radio stimulated more attention to the verbal soundtrack. To use McLuhan's terms, the ratio of the senses—auditory and visual—is different depending on the medium.

Thus far, I have treated the visual in contrast to the audio. But the key fact about television is that it is an audiovisual medium in which the two modes of expression are integrated. What sort of impact does this integration have on children? Research in England by Diane Jennings indicates that not until age seven does the addition of an audio track to a silent film add anything to children's immediate recall of a film.[15] Thus, visual information predominates over verbal early in life; the ability to integrate them in such a way that the whole is greater than the visual alone is a later step.

The issue of causality. What is not clear thus far is whether exposure to television *causes* the predominance of the visual sense or simply makes use of a naturally occurring stage of development. To put the question in McLuhan's terms, is television altering the ratio of children's senses in favor of the visual, or is it simply capitalizing on a pre-existing ratio?

Children develop their visual abilities very highly in the first year of life, before they acquire language. While they are in the process of learning language, they use this knowledge of the visual world to help them decode their mother tongue.[16] Hence, visual understanding of people, objects, and actions is an earlier and therefore more basic way of understanding the world than is language. A primacy of vision over language exists for television to exploit. And there is evidence that television does exploit it. As early as six months of age, infants will pay attention longer to a television set with a picture on the screen but no sound, than to a set emanating sound without any picture.[17]

One way of deciding if television does more than exploit a pre-existing ratio between vision and speech is to look at the way adults process visual and auditory information when the two are not in competition. If television *causes* the predominance of the visual, it should do so in adults as much as in children; the effect, if it is a function of exposure to television, should perhaps be even stronger in adults because they have had so much more experience with television over the course of their lives.

This question is addressed by a study in which some adults were shown a dialogueless movie, *The Red Balloon*, and others heard a tape-recorded narration of carefully matched episodes from the written story. Children in a parallel situation remember a silent film better than the soundtrack alone.[18] For adults, however, immediate recall of *The Red Balloon* was very similar in both media.[19] According to this study the predominance of the visual has disappeared with age. This indicates that television does not alter the ratio of the senses in a permanent way, but that in young children it makes use of a naturally occurring ratio that favors the visual at that particular stage of life. This is an important point in defense of television. While the sense of hearing may be less important in viewing television than in listening to radio or tape, television does not result in any long-term reduction of the importance of auditory stimuli in general.

Visual images and long-term memory. While the predominance of the visual over the auditory certainly decreases with age, it does not disappear altogether. Although the adults' immediate recall of *The Red Balloon* was not affected by medium, a second test seven days after the presentations showed that recall deteriorated faster for the participants who had heard the story than for those who had seen the film. Even for adults, visual memory proved to be more enduring than auditory memory. The significance of this finding is captured by a comment a friend of mine made about the film *My Dinner with Andre*, which has no visual action whatsoever, but simply records a long dinner-table conversation: "Everyone likes it, but no one remembers anything about it."

A film such as *E.T.* is at the opposite pole from *My Dinner with Andre*. It is a very visual film, nonverbal communication predominates, and there is little dialogue. This may be one of the sources of its great popularity among young children: it fits their own ratio of the senses, in which the visual predominates over the verbal. For older people, by contrast, especially people socialized with print and radio rather than television and film, this nonverbal quality may be distasteful.

THE INNER SENSE: IMAGINATION

In an interview, a retired baseball play-by-play radio broadcaster lamented the growth of television broadcasting for baseball, at the expense of radio. With radio, he said, the listener was an equal participant, an equal partner. The listener had to use imagination and memory, he continued, and it's a shame that that is lost.

Is there any truth to the idea that radio serves as a stimulus to the imagination? The claim is that the listener is an equal partner with the announcer because the listener has to contribute a mental image of the game as it is played, an image that involves memory and is personal to a particular member of the audience. This analysis implies that radio might stimulate the imagination more than television simply because it leaves more to the imagination.

Another study comparing radio and television was designed to test this idea with elementary school children. Again, each child was presented with one story in a radio format and a different one in a television format. But this time both stories were stopped a little bit before the end and the children were asked to continue them. The extent to which children introduced novel elements into their completions, elements that had not been in the story they had heard or seen, was the basis for our measures of imagination. Our basic finding was that children showed more imagination in their stories following radio than following television presentations. Thus, our results seem to provide scientific evidence for the belief voiced by the radio broadcaster that radio stimulates the imagination.[20]

The claim has been made that television actually depresses imaginative activity. For example Dorothy and Jerome Singer found in a study of preschool children that the more television a child watched, the less likely the child was to have an imaginary playmate (which they considered to be an index of imagination). Following the same children up to age eight, they found that heavy television watching, particularly action-adventure shows, continued to show an association with relatively low scores on imaginative play. A natural experiment in Canada showed that children's creativity, as measured by their ability to think of multiple uses for common objects, declined after the introduction of television into their town.[21]

However, the influences of the media on imagination are not so simple. For one thing, not all television has an adverse effect on imagination. Other work by the Singers points to the possibility that particular shows can stimulate imagination. They found that *Mr. Rogers*, a children's program that is unusual in its slow pace, pauses for the child to respond, and creation of a distinct fantasy world, stimulates make-believe play, particularly in less imaginative preschool children. *Sesame Street* has also been found to foster imaginative play in children initially low in imagination, although less so than *Mr. Rogers*. Another complexity is that certain imaginative or creative tasks do not seem to be negatively affected by television, while others do.[22]

Thus far I have been discussing verbal measures of imagination. But when people talk about imagination, they are often thinking specifically about visual imagery. Meringoff and colleagues investigated radio, television, and picture-book presentations to see what kind of visual images each stimulated. The researchers had the children draw pictures about the story. The radio version stimulated more imaginative drawings, in that children "chose a wider variety of story content to represent graphically and incorporated more extra-story content in their drawings."[23] However, if we consider not the originality of the drawings but their quality, then children exposed to television and the picture book did better. For example, they more often depicted characters from unusual perspectives, and they included more unusual details. This effect of television on drawing has also been observed in Scandinavia.[24] Thus, while television does not seem to foster as much variety or use of the child's prior experience in creating drawings as radio does, it does seem to foster visual skills, such as those required for the creation of visual perspective.

If radio stimulates the imagination more than television, it is because it leaves visual gaps for the listener to fill in from the imagination. Some background knowledge is often required for this purpose. In fact, children do use their own knowledge and experience more when interpreting a radio story than when interpreting a television story. It follows that a purely verbal presentation will have more meaning for a person who has the requisite knowledge and experience to use in interpreting it. Print, being a verbal medium, should also stimulate the imagination and the incorporation of the reader's own experience. And indeed, an experiment has found print to be equivalent to radio in stimulating imaginative thinking.[25]

In both reading and listening, when children lack the requisite background experience they may misinterpret the material. This can be a disadvantage in some situations, but it can also be a great advantage. If children read a book that goes beyond their experience in sex or violence, they may simply imagine it "wrong" or not at all. On television or film, in contrast, the same children, whether ready for the experience or not, will be forced to see it as it really is. Thus, the verbal media, by leaving so much to be filled in by the imagination, actually adjust to the level of the child listener or viewer. This is probably why no one worried about violence in books or radio the way they worry about it on television or in film, even though it may be present to the same degree.

After reading *Macbeth*, my daughter, Lauren, went to see Roman Polanski's film of the play. Although she had read about Macbeth's severed head at the end of the play, it was a shock to *see* it in the film. She commented that she had not realized there was so much violence in the play. Her response is probably similar to those of children studied in England twenty-five years ago: more than twice as many said they had been frightened by things they had seen on television or film than in reading or radio.[26] The visual realism of film or television is an advantage for learning new material. But it can also be a disadvantage, if the material goes beyond what the child is emotionally ready for or if the goal is to stimulate the child's own imagination.

IMPULSIVITY VERSUS REFLECTION AND PERSISTENCE

Television, in comparison with print, is often rapidly paced and always in continuous movement. It does not allow time for the viewer's own reflection. These qualities have led to speculation that television leads to an impulsive rather than reflective style of thought and to a lack of persistence in intellectual tasks. Evidence for this idea has been provided by a demonstration that restricting six-year-old children's television viewing decreases intellectual impulsiveness and increases reflectivity, as measured by a standard test.[27] A study in the United States found that heavy television viewing was associated with less ability to wait and more restlessness.[28] In Canada, adults in a town without television tended to be more persistent in problem-solving than adults from similar towns with television.[29]

All of these findings may reflect the fact that television, unlike print, must be processed at the pace of the program. There are always new stimuli that demand assimilation; the viewer has no time to persist in understanding the old ones. (The more widespread and creative use of video recorders may partially overcome this limitation, by allowing the viewer to stop a program, think about it, and even go over a part of it a second time.)

Note that these qualities apply to *all* television. I am not talking about differences in pacing *between* TV shows. There has been specific criticism of *Sesame Street* on this account, although *Sesame Street* in fact uses a variety of styles, some slow, some fast. Daniel Anderson tested the effect of pacing on reflectivity and task persistence. Fast-paced shows had frequent cuts, scene changes, and action of various sorts. Slow-paced shows did not. Using specially edited *Sesame Street* programs, Anderson found no effect of pacing on four-year-old children.[30] Television's reduction of reflectivity and persistence must stem not from particular techniques but from the universal fact that it is a medium that unfolds in real time. By virtue of this fact, it paces the viewer, rather than vice versa.

Print not only allows time for reflective thought in comparison with television or film, it also can portray thought much better than film can. For example, an important part of the book *Being There*, by Jerzy Kosinski, is made up of the thoughts of the main character, Chance. As my son, Matthew, has pointed out, the film version of *Being There* uses the TV screen to show the viewer what Chance is watching, but it is unable to portray the subtleties of what he is thinking. The predominance of television and film in children's media diet means that children are not being given models of reflective thought, for film is forced to portray internal thought through external action. This shortage of reflective models may be one reason why heavy television viewing seems to cause an impulsive style of thought and behavior.

IMPLICATIONS FOR EDUCATION AND SOCIALIZATION

More than the medium itself, it is the social context and use of a medium that determine the medium's impact on children's ways of thinking. Print in itself is merely a medium for transferring information; it is not a whole set of higher-level thinking skills. Print is probably a less efficient way to convey information, overall, than is television, with its dynamic visual images, which are more easily understood and remembered than are words.

Television should be used more in schools to communicate information. But it should be used with class discussion directed by the teacher. Children's ability to explain what they have seen on television may well depend on the teacher-pupil dialogue that surrounds the presentation. Like print, television and film are not substitutes for human interaction, but must be combined with and enhanced by it.

In terms of education and socialization, one medium's weakness is another medium's strength. While television has its value, the child also needs other experiences. Parents should restrict the amount of television their children watch at home in order to use other media and experiences to foster reflection and imagination. Encouraging children to read will enhance these types of thinking, while radio (or recordings if children's radio is not available) will stimulate imagination.

The skill of being articulate depends upon knowing how to be verbally explicit. This habit or skill is promoted more by the verbal media of print and radio, less by the audiovisual medium of television. Television seems to promote the use of nonverbal communication, which is also important. Again, a combination of media is desirable.

Because television is so powerful as a learning tool, it is all the more important that children be exposed to high-quality programming that (1) does not go beyond their emotional maturity and (2) provides fantasy or fact that will be useful, not detrimental, to life beyond the television set. How to improve the quality of television programming is a crucial topic, but one that is beyond the scope of this book. But as this chapter and earlier chapters have indicated, parents can do much to improve the effects of television by being selective about what shows children watch and by discussing programs to encourage the children to watch critically and thoughtfully.

7 / Video Games

In Glendale, California, a suburb of Los Angeles, I witnessed a scene that has recently been repeated in many parts of the United States. The City Council was hearing testimony about a proposed ordinance against video game arcades. These are establishments similar to old-fashioned pool halls, but featuring action games played on TV screens. A mother of two teenagers got up and complained that children use half their lunch money to play the games. The president of the Glendale Council of Parent-Teacher Associations pursued the same theme. In the most eloquent part of her emotional plea, the first speaker said, "It reminds me of smoking. Smoking doesn't do us any bit of good. We don't depend on it to live. And yet it's addictive and it's expensive, and this is what these games are . . . There are kids in there that really cannot stay away from them."

Let us go through this list of complaints and see what is known about each of them. First, are video games addictive? J. David Brooks interviewed 973 young people in video arcades in southern California. While he found some who felt compelled to play, they were in a minority. In fact, about half the kids were playing games less than half the time they were in the arcade. The rest of the time they were socializing. The arcades, like the

97

ice cream parlor of yore, were providing a social gathering place, more than a place for compulsive play.[1] In terms of management and physical environment, however, some arcades, unlike the old-fashioned ice cream parlor, are not healthy places for young people to gather. We should be concerned about regulating this aspect of the arcades in our communities.

In northern California, Edna Mitchell had twenty families keep diaries for one week each month for five months after getting a video game set. If the games were addictive (whatever that means), this should have been reflected in long hours spent playing, particularly since the games could be played at home without spending quarters. However, Mitchell found that the game sets were used an average of 42 minutes a day per *family*— and many families included more than one child, as well as parents who played.[2] This is hardly an addictive pattern, especially compared with the amount of time spent watching television. According to even the most conservative estimate, preschool children in the United States spend two and a half hours a day with the television set on.[3]

Second, how expensive are video games? Eighty percent of the kids interviewed by Brooks spent five dollars or less per week, the price of a movie. Only 7 percent spent lunch money. In fact, because they are better players, children put less money in the machines than adults do. In the world of video arcade games, skill is rewarded with play time, and a good player can play for an hour and a half on a quarter.

Finally, do the games "do us any bit of good"? The way to answer this question is to discover what skills are required by the games and what skills, therefore, the players might be developing. Here, I shall not limit myself to arcade games, but will also discuss other types of games that are available for home computers, as well as games that could become available in the future.

Thus, the available evidence indicates that video games are, in terms of time spent, much less addictive than television. Nor are they, in comparison with other entertainment, particularly expensive. Yet they are undeniably attractive, and there is something about that attraction that disturbs people. Before deciding that video games are bad simply because they are attractive, it makes sense to consider what features make them so attractive.

THE ATTRACTION OF VIDEO GAMES: THE TV CONNECTION

What makes computer games able to compete so successfully with the things children did before the games? As is by now common knowledge, television has in recent years been children's major waking activity. Video games have been dubbed the "marriage of television and the computer."[4] At the most obvious level, what television and computers have in common is a television screen, a cathode ray tube. Both use the screen to present visual motion. We saw in Chapter 3 that children with a television background develop a preference for dynamic visual imagery. And we learned that visual action is an important factor in attracting the attention of young children to the television screen. The popular arcade games involve a tremendous amount of visual action, and this may be one source of their appeal.

Thomas Malone analyzed the appeal of computer games, starting with a survey of the preferences of children who had become familiar with a wide variety of computer games in computer classes at a private elementary school in Palo Alto, California. The children ranged in age from about five to thirteen, and the games spanned the range from arcade games to simulations to adventure games to learning games. Visual elements were important in the games' popularity: graphics games such as Petball (computer pinball) and Snake 2 (two players controlling motion and shooting of snakes) were more popular than word games such as Eliza (conversation with a simulated psychiatrist) and Gold (a fill-in-the-blanks story about Goldilocks). A clue as to the attraction of *moving* visual images comes from the fact that the three most unpopular graphics games—Stars, Snoopy, and Draw—have no animation at all or much less animation than more popular games.[5]

If moving visual imagery is important in the popularity of video games, then perhaps the visual skills developed through watching television (documented in Chapters 2 and 3) are the reason children of the television generation show so much talent with the games. As discussed in Chapter 3, children also pick up and use more information about action from seeing action on television than from hearing action described (as in radio) or from verbal description combined with static images (as in picture books). Children who watch a lot of television get a great deal of experience in taking in information about action—more so than did generations socialized with the verbal media of print and radio. Perhaps this experience with the moving visual images of television leads to skills that can be applied to playing video games. I shall return to this possibility later when I analyze the skill requirements of the various games.

Video games have the dynamic visual element of television, but they are also interactive. What happens on the screen is not entirely determined by the computer; it is also very much influenced by the player's actions. A straightforward example is the original commercial computer game, Pong, an electronic ping-pong game. Like other popular computer games, Pong involves moving imagery, as television does. But instead of merely watching an animated ping-pong match, as one might watch Wimbledon on television, the player actually plays the match, and thus has a part in creating the video display.

It is possible that, before the advent of video games, a generation brought up on film and television was in a bind: the most active medium of expression, writing, lacked the quality of visual dynamism. Television had dynamism, but could not be affected by the viewer. Video games are the first medium to combine visual dynamism with an active participatory role for the child.

What evidence exists that a desire for interaction (in contrast to mere observation) is an important part of the appeal of computer games? No systematic research exists on this subject, to my knowledge, but studies have been done in other settings in which there are both things to observe and things to interact with, such as science museums, field trips, zoos, and aquariums. These studies show a predictable pattern: children are attracted to activities that let them become personally involved. In the zoo, for example, they prefer pigeons and squirrels, with whom they can interact, to the more exotic animals isolated behind bars.[6]

To get an idea of whether this finding applied to video games and of whether the games were displacing the one-way medium of television, I asked four children, ranging in age from eight to fourteen, what they used to do with the time they now spend on video games. In answer, three of the four mentioned television. Two of those three mentioned only television, the third a number of other activities, including playing games with friends. Information from my tiny sample is confirmed by Mitchell's larger study of families with home video game sets; the children in her sample also watched less television after getting their game machines.

I also asked my four interviewees which they liked better, TV or video games, and why. They were unanimous in preferring the games to television. They were also unanimous about the reason: active control. The meaning of control was both very concrete and very conscious. One nine-year-old girl said, "In TV, if you want to make someone die, you can't. In Pac-Man, if you want to run into a ghost you can." Another girl of the same age said, "On TV you can't say 'shoot now' or, with Popeye, 'eat your spinach now.' " She went on to say she would get frustrated sometimes watching Popeye and wanting him to eat his spinach at a certain time when he didn't.

OTHER REASONS FOR THE APPEAL OF VIDEO GAMES

One of the children I interviewed mentioned playing games with friends as an activity she used to do more before video games. If video games are in fact displacing more traditional games as well as television, then the question arises, what are the elements that make computer games more attractive than other sorts of games? Perhaps the most obvious and important comparison is between computer games and the indoor games that existed before them: board games like checkers and monopoly, card games, tic-tac-toe. (Even though these games now exist in computer form, they were not, of course, developed for the computer medium.)

Malone found that the presence of a goal was the single most important factor in determining the popularity of games. This is a quality that arcade games share with all true games. Other qualities he found to enhance the popularity of computer games were automatic score-keeping, audio effects, randomness (the operation of chance), and the importance of speed. Of these qualities, randomness (as in games controlled by dice) and speed (as in double solitaire) are part of some conventional games. The others, automatic scorekeeping and audio effects, are essentially impossible without electronics.

THE PROBLEM OF VIOLENCE

If dynamic visual graphics, sound effects, and automatic scorekeeping are the features that account for the popularity of video games, why are parents so worried? All of these features seem quite innocent. But another source of concern is that the games available in arcades have, almost without exception, themes of physical aggression. Daniel Anderson points out the parallels with other media: "Video games have violent content; TV has violent content; comic books had violent content; movies had (have) violent content. There has long been the belief that violent content may teach violent behavior. And yet again our society finds a new medium in which to present that content, and yet again the demand is nearly insatiable."[7] And there is evidence that violent video games breed violent behavior, just as violent television shows do: both Space Invaders and Roadrunner have been found to raise the level of aggressive play (and lower the level of prosocial play) in five-year-old children; interestingly enough, they do so to the same degree.[8]

The effects of video violence are less simple, however, than they at first appeared. The same group of researchers who found these negative effects of Roadrunner and Space Invaders have more recently found that two-player aggressive video games, whether cooperative or competitive, reduce the level of aggression in children's play. (In this study, both the competitive and the cooperative games were violent. It is notable that playing the violent but cooperative game neither decreased nor increased subsequent cooperative behavior.)[9]

It may be that the most harmful aspect of the violent video games is that they are solitary in nature. A two-person aggressive game (video boxing, in this study) seems to provide a cathartic or releasing effect for aggression, while a solitary aggressive game (such as Space Invaders) may stimulate further aggression. Perhaps the effects of television in stimulating aggression will also be found to stem partly from the fact that TV viewing typically involves little social interaction.

With or without social interaction, violent content is certainly not a necessary feature of video games. It does not even seem necessary to the games' popularity. The most popular game in Malone's survey was Petball, a version of computer pinball, a game that has no obvious aggression in it at all. (Computer pinball does, however, have all of the qualities that distinguish computer games from conventional indoor games.) Similarly, Breakout, the number three game, has a relatively mild aggressive theme (balls knocking a brick wall down); it was more popular than more violent games such as Mission, which involves bombing submarines, and Star Wars, which consists of shooting at Darth Vader's ship.

These rankings indicate that the popularity of computer games does not depend on violence, but on other features that can be used with both violent and nonviolent themes. Ironically enough, the same message comes from recent television research: action, not violence in itself, is what attracts young children to the screen.[10] It follows that programs can present many forms of action other than violent action without sacrificing popularity. There is a clear message for the manufacturers of video games: they should forsake violence because of its undesirable social consequences; they can use other action themes without sacrificing the popularity of the games.

Indeed, some children are actually alienated from arcade games *because* of the aggressive themes. Malone analyzed the appeal of Darts, a game designed to teach fractions to elementary school children. The left side of figure 4 shows the basic display on the screen. The child must try to guess the position of the balloons by typing in a mixed number (whole number and fraction) specifying each balloon's position on the number line. If the answer is right, an arrow comes shooting across the screen and pops the balloon. If it is wrong, the arrow shoots across to the number line and remains there as permanent feedback about the error. Thus, the game has a mildly aggressive fantasy theme. Malone created several versions of this game, each one lacking one or more features of the original. Two such versions are shown in the middle and right-hand sides of figure 4. Adding the aggressive fantasy (right side of illustration) to a version without a theme (middle of illustration) increased its popularity among boys but decreased it among girls. In short, the aggressive fantasy was a turn-on for the boys but a turn-off for the girls.

This sex difference has important social implications. In the crowds around game machines, boys far outnumber girls. This may be a serious problem, because it appears that games are the entry point into the world of computers for most children. If children's interest in computers begins with games, then the fact that the most common computer games involve aggressive and violent fantasy themes may have the effect of turning

4. *Three Darts displays. The basic game is on the left. The version on the right differs from the one in the middle in including an element of aggressive fantasy. (Adapted from Malone, "Toward a Theory of Intrinsically Motivating Instruction.")*

many girls away from computers in general. This would be especially unfortunate in a field that is still in rapid growth and therefore should be especially promising for women. There is an urgent need for widely available video games that make as firm contact with the fantasy life of the typical girl as with that of the typical boy. (There does seem to be a trend in this direction with the addition to arcades of less violent games, such as Donkey Kong, that are more popular with girls.)[11]

Nothing intrinsic to video games requires one theme rather than another. The same formal features can be embodied in a myriad of themes. For example, as Tom Malone pointed out to me, the aggressive game of Space Invaders is formally similar to the basically nonviolent game of Breakout. Children's Computer Workshop, a division of Children's Television Workshop, is creating educational software with action game formats and nonviolent themes. One that has been developed is Taxi, a game where the goal is to drive a passenger through a city as quickly and efficiently as possible, overcoming obstacles on the way. Taxi has the action and high-speed appeal of an arcade game without the violent content.

Another important point about this and other games being developed by the Workshop is that, besides being nonviolent, they can be played cooperatively with another person. Leona Schauble, the director of Children's Computer Workshop, reports that, in play tests of Taxi, children became increasingly cooperative as they became experienced with the game and learned that cooperation paid off. Like television, the medium of video games is in itself neutral with respect to social values. Nevertheless, the choice of a game design can have an important influence on children's behavior.

THE SKILLS OF VIDEO GAMES

Another concern about video games is that they are merely sensorimotor games of eye-hand coordination and that they are therefore mindless. I take issue with that proposition on two grounds. First, sensorimotor skills such as eye-hand coordination are important in themselves. They are useful in many occupations, as well as in everyday life, and according to Piaget's theory they are the foundation for later stages of cognitive development.

Second, it turns out that there is much more to the games than eye-hand coordination. In fact not only are they complex, they incorporate types of complexity that are impossible with conventional games. I am convinced that many of the people who criticize the games would not be able to play them themselves, and that their problems would be more than just those of eye-hand coordination. Let me illustrate with the game of Pac-Man.

Pac-Man. When I played Pac-Man for the first time, I had watched it played quite a number of times, and I assumed I would be able to play it myself, even if not with consummate skill. But when I started, I found I could not even distinguish Pac-Man, whom I was supposed to control, from the other blobs on the screen! A little girl of about five had to explain the game to me.

On a later play, I decided that I had so much trouble finding Pac-Man that first time because when Pac-Man first appears in the complex array of blobs and dots he does not have a wedged-shaped piece cut out of him; he is simply a yellow circle. I think that, as a person socialized into the world of static visual information, I made the unconscious assumption that Pac-Man would not change visual form. My hypothesis is that children socialized with television and film are more used to dealing with dynamic visual change and are less likely to make such a limiting assumption.

After trying the game again, I thought I had the basics. True, my score was not very good, but I assumed that was because my reflexes were not fast and I lacked sensorimotor practice. A few months later I bought *The Video Master's Guide to Pac-Man* in the hopes of finding out something about the psychology of video games. I was amazed to discover that I had missed all but the most obvious aspects of the game. Pac-Man is much more complex than I had imagined. Furthermore, most of the complexities are of a sort that cannot be incorporated in conventional board games such as checkers, chess, or monopoly. True, Pac-Man is an action game and therefore requires a certain amount of eye-hand coordination, but that is only the beginning of the game, not the end.

I am convinced that the people who criticize video games do not understand what the games involve. As I found out to my chagrin, a game like Pac-Man is not something one can pick up by standing around a machine for a few minutes, watching someone else play. I will describe Pac-Man in some detail in order to analyze the learning and cognitive processes that one must go through to become a skilled player.

When a player inserts a quarter into the Pac-Man machine, a maze filled with white dots appears on the screen (see figure 5). In the middle of the lower half of the screen appears Pac-Man, a yellow circle. The player uses the control stick to guide Pac-Man (now with open wedge-shaped mouth) through the maze. As Pac-Man encounters each white dot he "eats" it and it disappears; the object is to clear the maze of dots by having Pac-Man eat them all.

Thus far, the game seems simple enough, and it can be played at the level of this basic description. This was

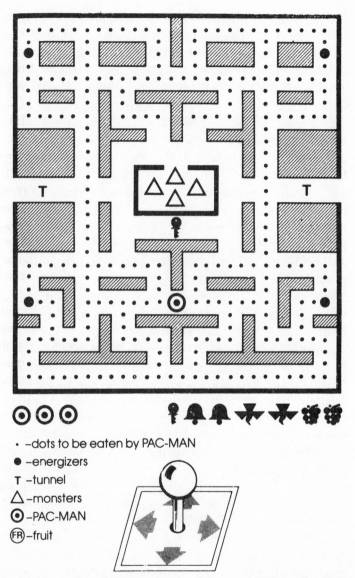

- -dots to be eaten by PAC-MAN
- -energizers
T -tunnel
△ -monsters
⊙ -PAC-MAN
(FR) -fruit

5. *Pac-Man game board layout.* (*From Sykora and Birkner,* The Video Master's Guide to Pac-Man.)

probably about the level at which I played it at first. As in all games, however, there are obstacles. In Pac-Man the obstacles are not physical barriers but four monsters or ghosts, which chase Pac-Man through the maze and eat him if they catch him. Each monster has its own characteristic behavior. For example, the red monster, Shadow, is the most aggressive. The pink one, Speedy, the fastest monster, usually does not chase Pac-Man for very long at one time but does tend to come after him fairly often. The third monster, Pokey, will not cross any of the energizers. (The energizers are four large blinking dots. Each time Pac-Man eats an energizer, he is awarded fifty points and for a few seconds he becomes more powerful than the monsters, so that he can chase and eat them. For each monster he devours he gets more points.)[12]

This situation may sound a bit like chess, in which each piece has its own allowed behavior. But in Pac-Man, as in other video games, no one tells the player the rules governing each monster's behavior; these rules must be induced from observation. In this way, Pac-Man is more like life than like chess. The player must not only overcome the obstacles but must also perform the inductive task of figuring out the nature of the obstacles. The behavior patterns the player must discover lie in the game's computer program. Rick Sinatra, a computer programmer, may have had this aspect of the games in mind when he remarked: "Video games are revolutionary; they are the beginnings of human interaction with artificial intelligence."

As another obvious source of complexity, the arcade-style video games, unlike board games, have real-time movement in them. In chess or checkers the player moves pieces around a board, but the movement itself is not part of the game. Timing does not count. In Pac-Man, by contrast, quickness is vital as the player tries to keep Pac-Man away from the monsters.

Further complexity comes from the nature of the maze. It looks simple; there are no blind alleys or cul-de-sacs, complications of the conventional precomputer maze. However, the Pac-Man maze has complications of a different sort, which would not be possible without computer technology. The possibilities for movement are not uniform throughout the maze, even though the terrain all looks the same. The relative speeds of the monsters and Pac-Man are different in different parts of the maze, so that the monsters can overtake Pac-Man in the labyrinthine parts but not on the straightaways. In addition, there are some areas of the maze where Pac-Man can enter much more easily than the monsters and which therefore provide Pac-Man with relative safety. Such movement-related constraints simply do not exist in conventional games. These invisible complexities are programmed into the game's microcomputer.

Note that, as with the behavior of the monsters, the player does not know these spatial contingencies before starting to play. Whereas a conventional board game gives you all the rules, Pac-Man and other arcade-type computer games require the player to induce the rules from observation. Computer games therefore call up inductive skills much more than did games of the precomputer era.

Without this inductive effort, the games seem to be something like gambling games, in which a player deals with primarily random events. My son, Matthew, said of Pac-Man, "At first it was thought to be incredibly hard. Then people realized it wasn't random and figured out the patterns." Matthew also confirmed the existence of the inductive process: by watching others and then playing yourself, he said, "You just learn what things

have what characteristics and what they do." An idea
of the rate of learning is revealed in a saying among
players: "You spend fifteen or twenty dollars on a game.
Then you can play an hour and a half for a quarter."
Part of the excitement of the games surely must lie in
this process of transforming randomness into order
through induction. (Adults may not learn as quickly; a
bartender who had games in his bar estimated that it
typically cost one of his customers a hundred dollars to
get his name in the top five.)

Pac-Man also illustrates another cognitive require-
ment of skillful video game playing: parallel processing.
As discussed in Chapter 3, this term refers to taking in
information from several sources simultaneously; it contrasts with serial processing, in which the mind takes
in information from one source at a time. In Pac-Man,
to be a good player, you must simultaneously keep track
of Pac-Man, the four monsters, where you are in the
maze, and the four energizers. Many other games have
even more information sources that must be dealt with
simultaneously.

Here the skills and habits developed by watching much
television may be very useful. Pictorial images in general
tend to elicit parallel processing,[13] while verbal media,
because of the sequential nature of language (you read
or hear one word at a time), tend to elicit serial processing. In television there are frequently several things
happening on the screen simultaneously. In Chapter 2
I gave an example from *Hill Street Blues* of how plot
development can use this formal characteristic of the
medium; Robert Altman's film *Nashville* provides a similar example. Consequently, a child whose main media
background was television, rather than print or radio,
could be more prepared for the parallel processing de-
manded by skillful video game playing.

Pac-Man embodies another cognitive complexity that

was impossible in precomputer games: the interaction of two elements yields results that could not be predicted from either one separately. Thus, if you watched Pac-Man's behavior alone, you could not discover the special qualities of different parts of the maze. Nor could you by watching the monsters' behavior alone. Even inspection of the maze itself gives no clue. Only by watching the monsters interacting with Pac-Man in different parts of the maze can you detect the dynamic qualities of the maze.

This quality of interacting dynamic variables characterizes just about all computer action games. In fact, it exists in about the simplest form possible in Pac-Man. This simplicity is handy for getting across the concept of interacting variables to people who may not be familiar with computer games, but it hardly scratches the surface of the cognitive complexity that expert players of the more difficult games (for example, Defender) have to deal with.

Tranquility Base. Let me give an example of complex interacting dynamic variables from an action game that has more educational content. The game, called Tranquility Base, is similar to Moon Lander, a computer game found in a number of children's museums and science centers around the United States. The object of the game is to land a space ship without crashing it. There are six basic variables involved: altitude, vertical speed, horizontal speed, direction, amount of fuel, and terrain (the same as horizontal location). The player controls thrust (acceleration) and horizontal direction. Each of the variables interacts with the others in complex ways. In order to land the spaceship safely, the player must take account of the variables not only one at a time but also as they influence one another. As I tried to learn the game, I found myself wanting to deal with one variable at a time. When that proved impossible, I tried dealing with them simultaneously, but as independent, rather than interacting, variables. That was no more successful. I worked for over an hour without making one successful landing. Matthew, who had taught me the game, strategy as well as basics, was frustrated with me. He could not understand why I was having so much trouble. Clearly, the strategy of integrating the interacting variables had become second nature to him. This may well be an important skill that video players are acquiring through practice with the games.

Experimental work confirms that games that require the player to induce the relations among multiple interacting variables are difficult for many people. Learning to play this type of game, furthermore, brings out important skills such as flexibility and an orientation toward independent achievement.[14] These skills are not called into play either by simpler games in which the variables do not interact or by games in which the player is told all the rules in advance. This is, I think, an important finding. Learning to deal with multiple interacting variables is a significant accomplishment because the world is not a simple system, but rather many complex systems of multiple interacting factors. But how much transfer can we expect from video games to other domains of knowledge and life?

The issue of transfer. Such transfer from the games to other domains cannot be taken for granted; it is far from automatic. As we saw in Chapter 6 with the example of literacy, transfer from a medium to a skill is not just a question of basic knowledge of the medium, but depends on how the medium is used.

Transfer of concepts to a new domain often seems to require their verbal formulation; yet the knowledge gained in playing video games is more than likely nonverbal. We saw earlier that verbal explanation is fostered by the dialogue between teacher and student that typically goes on in school. The transfer and generalization of the formal knowledge gained in playing video games may therefore depend on bringing the games into the school, not necessarily to play them, but to make them an object of study and discussion. An example of this will be presented in Chapter 9.

Spatial skills. Spatial skills are another area of cognitive skills that many computer games require and therefore must promote as players become more skilled. Michael Williams first suggested this idea to me, using the example of Star Raiders. Star Raiders presents three-dimensional information in two dimensions, using conventions of perspective. Thus, in order to play the game well, the player must be skilled at interpreting these conventions. This skill is required by a number of popular games besides Star Raiders, such as Zaxxon.

Many computer games require the ability to coordinate visual information coming from multiple perspectives. This is a skill emphasized in Piaget's account of intellectual development. For example, Tranquility Base involves a very simple coordination of perspectives (see figure 6). As the game begins, the player sees a long view of the space ship and the terrain where it is to land (top of illustration). As the ship gets closer to the ground, the view shifts to a close-up of the particular section of terrain that has been chosen for landing (bottom of illustration). It is a bit like what a pilot would see as a plane (or spaceship) approached the earth.

Castle Wolfenstein is a game for home computers that involves a more complex coordination of perspectives. It is a chase game with an anti-Nazi theme that takes place in a series of mazes. Although the mazes are in two dimensions, they are meant to be part of a three-dimensional prison. The storeys of the prison are linked by visible stairs, whose position serves as the visual cue for coordinating the individual mazes into a three-di-

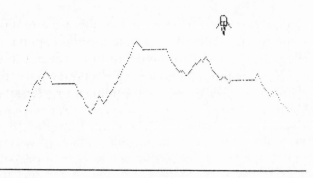

6. *Two screens from Tranquility Base: top, long shot; bottom, close-up view.*

mensional layout. In addition, each storey consists of more than one maze. Parts of a single storey are linked by doors, which, like the stairs, serve as cues for integrating individual mazes into the layout of a given storey.

When Matthew taught me how to play this game, I completely missed the aspect of spatial integration. I treated the mazes as if they were independent. I was totally unaware that the mazes were linked in the third dimension through stairs. I even missed the connections between mazes on the same level and did not realize that to leave a maze by the same door by which I entered was to go backward to an earlier maze instead of advancing to a new one. Matthew commented, "Most peo-

ple realize *that* even if they are not paying attention."
Apparently, the ability to integrate different spatial perspectives has become automatic in him, but not in me.
This anecdote cannot tell us anything about what caused
the difference, whether it is the male's greater spatial
ability, practice in playing the games at a relatively young
age, familiarity with particular game formats, a foundation of visual skills developed through watching television, or all of these together. But it does indicate that
spatial integrative skills are involved in playing the game
and that such skills cannot be taken for granted.

Recall from Chapter 2 that the ability to coordinate
information from more than one visual perspective is
one of the skills that Israeli children developed through
watching *Sesame Street.* Perhaps this skill, first developed through watching television, is later helpful to a
child playing a video game such as Castle Wolfenstein.

The suspicion that visual-spatial skills could be useful
with and developed by video games was reinforced in
my mind when I noticed that almost every child at the
computer camp Matthew attended in the summer of
1981 came equipped with the Rubik's cube. Some of the
campers had computer experience; some did not. But
virtually all were experienced video game players. Not
only did they have cubes, as many children did at that
time, but the majority of them could solve the cube,
some with amazing speed. (There were regular contests,
not to see *if* you could do it, but how fast!) It seemed
to me that this group of video game aficionados had
more interest and skill with the cube than would be
found in children with no experience with video games.
My hypothesis is that Rubik's cube and video games
demand and develop some of the same visual-spatial
skills.

The culture gap was impressed upon me when I found
that I not only was unable to do the cube but also could

not understand my son's patient explanation, even accompanied by demonstration. The very terminology and frame of reference made no contact with anything familiar to me. It was as if he were speaking a foreign language. Clearly, I lacked some sort of spatial conceptualization required for the cube. Perhaps this lack of spatial skills is one element in my great difficulty with video games.

Fantasy games. Not all computer games are action games. Another important type of game is the fantasy adventure game. Until very recently games of this type have not been available in arcades, but only as programs for home computers. Fantasy games involve complex characters with a medieval flavor who go on adventures together and meet a wide variety of circumstances and obstacles. This type of game has a number of interesting features that separate it from traditional games.

One distinguishing mark of this type of game is that there are so many more possible happenings and characters than in a traditional game. Events are constrained by rules, but the constraints are much broader than in traditional games; in this way the games are more like life. Another interesting feature is that characters are multidimensional. In the game of Wizardry, for example, the characters are composed of different combinations of six qualities—strength, IQ, luck, agility, vitality, and piety—in addition to belonging to unidimensional categories, as chess pieces do. (Rather than kings, queens, pawns, and so on, the categories in Wizardry are fighters, priests, gnomes, and so on.) The characters also have complex and varying combinations of external qualities, notably armor, weapons, gold, and spells. Thus, to play such games well, children have to understand and construct multidimensional character structure.

Another interesting feature is that the characters are created by the player. Within certain constraints, qualities are chosen rather than assigned. Thus, the games stimulate creative thinking in the players. Also, there is more character development than in conventional games. For example, characters gain "experience points" as they go through adventures, and their capabilities change as a function of this experience. Characters can be "saved" on computer disk, so that this development can continue over a period of time and continuous progress can be made. Thus, the fantasy games are not only more complex in some ways than conventional games, they are also more dynamic. The player is stimulated to develop or use concepts of character development.

Other examples of creativity. Eric Wanner has suggested that video games could be much more interesting if they provided for more creation, particularly the creation that comes with programming.[15] While it is true that arcade games are totally preprogrammed, the fantasy games, available for home computers, do involve a certain amount of creation. Even more open-ended and creative is a game like the Pinball Construction Set (see figure 7), where you first build your own pinball alley, manipulating its geometry, physics, and electrical wiring as well as the placement of its flippers, bumpers, and so on. Then you play the pinball game you have created. Thus, creative and constructive abilities, as well as the playing abilities of a traditional game, are called into play. The computer makes it possible for video games to have this creative and open-ended aspect.

Going one step further in this direction are games that incorporate programming into a game format. In Robot Wars, for example, the player first programs a robot to behave in certain ways. Each player creates his or her own robot through programming. This type of game seems to combine the excitement of control and creation (when the program works) with the motivation of a goal-oriented game.

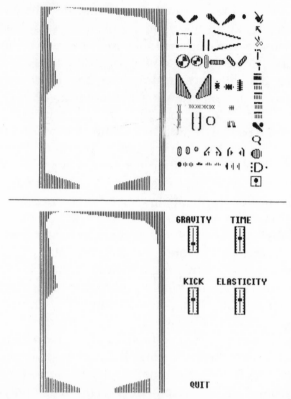

7. *Two screens from Pinball Construction Set. Both contain the basic alley. The top screen shows the various parts the player can use in constructing the game: flippers, bumpers, targets, and so on. The bottom screen contains dials for adjusting the physical variables of the game: the player can decrease or increase gravity, the speed of the simulation, the kicking strength of bumpers, and the elasticity (resilience) of collisions between balls and alley surfaces.*

As Wanner points out, it is a shame that the more imaginative and creative types of games are not available to the general public, those who are able to spend quarters but not bigger money on computer technology. Perhaps the invasion of schools by computers will make these creative games, as well as the computer experiences I will describe in the next chapter, available on a much broader scale. Although this is bound to happen to some extent, inequities in school ownership of computers based on social class of the school's population has already arisen, putting poorer children at a disadvantage in this area, as in others.[16]

A LADDER OF CHALLENGES

One more general characteristic of video games is, I believe, an important contributor to their learning potential. This is the fact that almost all the games have different levels, geared to the player's skill. In Pac-Man, after the player has cleared the dots on one maze, a new maze appears on the screen with more difficult characteristics. For example, in later stages of the game, Pac-Man cannot eat the monsters, even after having been "energized"; he can only force their retreat. A series of levels should have several effects. First, moving to a new level is a tangible sign of progress. Secondly, each new level presents a new challenge. And finally, having multiple levels introduces great variety into the game and creates curiosity as to what the next level will be like.

Evidence from work with learning-disabled children in an after-school educational setting emphasizes the appeal of levels of increasing difficulty. A game called Space Eggs, for instance, had such multiple levels. As they became expert players of Space Eggs, children kept moving from level to level, discovering new properties as they did so. "The day finally came, however, when one child achieved to the degree that the computer had no further response to: all that happens is that the most complex pattern repeats itself. The child's response was simple: he stopped playing the game. During future days at computer time, he chose other games, going back to Space Eggs only rarely."[17] It seems that far from being lazy or seeking mindless games, children look for games that challenge them.

Video games and learning-disabled children. The same study of learning-disabled children found that the arcade games were in many ways better educational tools for learning-disabled children than "educational" games or education in general. Children who avoid instruction during reading time were willing to be instructed during computer time. Some children who refused to concentrate on conventional learning tasks concentrated very well on the arcade-style games, showing perseverance and making a great deal of progress from trial to trial. The children also began to act as teachers of their peers and of adults. They would ask one another how to get a game started or how to play, and expert players would coach novices in the game's advanced strategies. Here is a case where computer technology removes handicaps that impede progress in other areas of education.

Multiple levels and addiction. According to Malone's study, the existence of multiple levels does not affect the popularity of particular games. But as the anecdote about Space Eggs shows, this characteristic may well affect *how long* a game remains interesting and popular, as well as how much is learned from it.

The existence of multiple levels may also be responsible for the addictive properties of the games claimed by the Glendale mother at the beginning of this chapter. A video game player makes visible progress in the form of improved score and reaching the next level. Yet there is always another level to master. The challenge of ever-new game conditions, added to the feeling of control that children claim computer games give them, creates a long-term appeal. As Malone has pointed out, learning situations other than computer games ought to be able to incorporate these powerful motivational features. Perhaps the most valuable thing we can learn is not how to make the games less addictive but how to make other learning experiences, particularly school, more so.

GAMES OF THE FUTURE

The motivating features of video games are beginning to be put to more explicit educational use. For example, Rocky's Boots, designed for home computers, uses a game format to teach the logic of computer circuitry. Early research findings indicate that players are engrossed by the game and learn from it. In Green Globs the player writes equations to hit randomly placed globs with a plotted curve, making progress in analytic geometry in moving from level to level.[18]

James Levin and Yaakov Kareev have suggested some imaginative possibilities for future games. A video game always creates its own microworld, and they point out that game designers could structure these worlds to reflect knowledge we want the players to acquire. For example, they describe a "chemical adventure" game that could be designed to teach about the periodic table of elements:

> Suppose that in a game world, we personify elements as people having characteristics analogous to their namesake elements. So we would have the muscle men Chromium, Manganese, and Iron, the attractive Chlorine, Fluorine, and Iodine, the casanovas Lithium, Sodium and Potassium, the super rich Platinum, Gold, Silver, and Copper. A goal in this game might be to rescue Silver, who is being held hostage by the seductive Chlorine (the compound silver chloride, used in photographic paper) . . . the player could use a magic powder (free electrons) to sprinkle over Silver to reduce his attraction to Chlorine, so that he can be set free . . . along

the way the player would have to avoid the dangerous Arsenic and Plutonium, distracting Arsenic with Gallium, or using Lead as a shield from Plutonium's rays . . . This sketch of a chemical adventure points to the ways that a computer game program could draw upon the same aspects that make current adventures entertaining, yet teach an abstract knowledge domain.[19]

Video games are a new medium, and scientific study of them is just beginning. Most of my discussion of skills involved in the games has been based on analyses of the games themselves, plus a few observations of individual cases. Such analyses furnish but a starting point for the systematic research of the future. More important, while this type of analysis can give important clues as to the skill involved in playing the games, it cannot tell us how far these skills transfer to situations outside the game itself. Just as is the case for other media, the games may well have to be used in an instructional context, with guidance and discussion by teachers, for the important skills to transfer very far. We should not forget, however, that knowledge and skill can be of value in themselves even if they are not transferable to new situations.

In thinking about video games, we should not think only of the shoot-'em-up space games that predominate in the arcade. There are, and there can be, a wide variety of game formats that utilize the marriage of computer and television. Because it can be programmed, the computer is a highly flexible medium, and the possibilities are endless.

As with any medium, the medium of video games has its own pattern of strengths and weaknesses. This medium may include more variation than most, however. For example, the real-time action games may foster parallel processing skills and fast reaction time but may also discourage reflection. (If you stop to think while playing Space Invaders, you're lost.) By contrast, games with a verbal format (for example, some of the fantasy-adventure games) use serial processing and allow unlimited time for reflection and planning. The real danger may be in the very variety, complexity, and appeal of game worlds that are so responsive to the child's input. As Karen Sheingold has speculated, too much control over the fantasy worlds of video games could bring about impatience with the messy, uncontrollable world of real life. This possible danger must, however, be weighed against the positive effects of achievement and control for children who, for whatever reasons, lack a sense of competence and predictability in other domains of life.

8 / Computers

Computer circuitry that in the 1960s would have cost hundreds of thousands of dollars and taken up roomfuls of space can now be made for less than a dollar and has been miniaturized to a quarter of an inch. Corresponding to these changes, there has been a dramatic increase in the availability of small computers to the general public. Children seem to be particularly attracted to this technology. Video games have become a mass (and very controversial) activity. In a time of limited budgets, schools have been purchasing computers like mad; more than half of all schools in the United States now have them.[1] Computer camps have sprung up all over the country, and many children (18 percent in California, according to an estimate by the California Department of Education)[2] have computers available at home—not just game machines but real programmable computers. Thus, computers have become an important medium in the lives of children.

THE TELEVISION CONNECTION

As with video games, part of the reason computers are so attractive to children may be children's experience with television. The link between television and computers appears to be noticed by children themselves. In a series of interviews done for a film about computers and children, one child said of computers: "It's like learning and watching a television at the same time." Others mentioned differences between television and the computer closely related to the differences between television and video games I mentioned in the previous chapter. For example, one boy said, "TV, it does what it wants to do. A computer does what you want it to." Another child's comment was similar: "It's fun because you get to control it. TV controls itself." Television has been accused of depressing the imagination; one boy saw computers as being different from television in this respect: "With TV you don't have to talk; you don't have to picture anything in your head."[3]

The children were unanimous in their preference for computers over television, just as the children I interviewed preferred video games to TV. (Children interviewed in the film had used computers for games, as well as for other functions in their classroom.)

The psychological interrelatedness of television and computers was first impressed upon me at home. When we got a home computer, the amount of time my son spent watching television decreased markedly. A case study of two other children, done by Yaakov Kareev, confirmed my observation.[4] A possible interpretation of this is that children love the visual dynamism of television, but that they prefer an interactive participatory role to a passive one. This is basically an extension of my argument in the last chapter from video games to computers in general.

Dean Brown, a pioneer in the development of computer technology, has called the computer the most astounding invention because of its unique combination of features: it is (1) dynamic, (2) interactive, and (3) programmable.[5] Unlike print, radio has auditory dynamism; it can present sound in real time with all its dynamic qualities. Television and film add the quality of visual dynamism. However, they are neither interactive nor programmable. The computer builds upon the dynamism of television, but adds these two qualities.

The interactive quality of the computer can be illustrated very simply with video games: the player affects what happens on the screen, and developments on the screen, in turn, constrain the possibilities for the player's next move. Thus, control and influence over the game go in two directions, from the player and from the computer. The same is true of computer-assisted instruction, where, at the simplest level, the computer poses the problem, the learner responds, and the computer gives feedback specific to that response. In a slightly more complex learning program, the learner's response can influence the choice of the next problem. As in video games, the computer provides a two-way street.

The third quality of computers, programmability, comes into play mainly with the activity of computer programming. Again, the attraction for children may grow out of their television experience. Herbert Kohl comments on what children choose to program :"I have found that the ability to compose music, develop visual images, animate figures, and control color effects are the most compelling aspects of programming for young people. In this way they can turn the tables on TV. They make their own programs instead of passively receiving someone else's."[6]

Three important uses of computer technology with children are learning software, word processing, and programming. All three take advantage of the interactive quality of the computer. However, they differ in the amount of control they allow the child user. With learning software, the computer, while responsive to the child, is definitely in charge: the computer programs the child (although the degree to which this is so varies from program to program). In word processing, the computer program furnishes a tool,[7] and the child both creates the material—text—upon which the tool works and decides how to use the tool to shape the material. In programming, the child tells the computer what to do, using a special language the computer can understand.

LEARNING SOFTWARE

Computer-Assisted Instruction. Although the line between video games and learning software has become increasingly blurred over time, the original learning programs were drill and practice programs developed under the rubric of Computer-Assisted Instruction (CAI). These programs, developed before current computer technology with its animated graphics, are essentially question-and-answer programs in which the computer poses the problem, gives the student a chance to respond, and then tells the student if the answer is right. With children, such programs are generally effective as supplements to traditional instruction, in mathematics and language arts for example.[8]

The major limitation of these programs is that they are more suited to provide practice in skills that are already present than to teach something new. Therefore, they tend to work best with students who already possess the basic skills in question. An example of this comes from a study in which a battery of drill and practice programs in math, reading, and language arts were tried out in a systematic way in elementary schools in Los Angeles.[9] Drill and practice in mathematics, where students already had basic concepts, were considerably more effective than drill and practice in reading: some students could not read well enough to gain much from the reading program. The computer drills could help them practice reading, but they could not teach them to read. This distinction is not a hard and fast one. Drill and practice can be used efficiently to teach certain types of knowledge, such as vocabulary, that lend themselves to a multiple-choice format.

The Los Angeles study was done in an economically disadvantaged group of children, and although the drill and practice programs were more effective for some subjects than for others, children who used the computer for drill and practice did better in certain aspects of all subjects than other children from the same school who did not use the computer. This illustrates an important theme that emerges again and again: like television, computer-based learning is not only effective in middle-class environments; it also works for children from educationally disadvantaged homes. Like the earlier electronic media, computers seem to work equally well with people from a wide variety of backgrounds. Computers are also effective tools for teaching children with various learning handicaps.[10] It seems clear that computers can reach children who have not been reached by older and more traditional educational methods.

Drill and practice programs utilize relatively little that is unique to the computer. Basically, they simulate a workbook type of situation. But they do have two advantages directly attributable to the computer: individualization of questions depending on the learner's level of skill, and instantaneous feedback.

The computer's feedback is not only instantaneous; it is also totally impersonal. This is an advantage from a psychological point of view: error becomes something to learn from rather than to fear. As a seven-year-old put it, "The computer doesn't yell." Nor does it have favorites. Indeed, computer technology lowers both the real and the psychological cost of error in all areas it touches, not just in drill-and-practice software. This is important because many negative patterns of behavior in school grow out of fear of error and fear of failure.[11]

Teaching with models. Another category of learning program makes use of even more of the computer's unique capacities. This category involves model-building of one sort or another. A very simple example of using a model to teach is the game of Harpoon, designed by James Levin, in which the goal is to specify the position of a shark by estimating points on two number lines, one horizontal and one vertical. "The program asks the players to specify the position of the shark left and right and then its position up and down. After they enter the two numbers, a 'harpoon' flies across the screen to the position they have specified. If that spot is close enough to the shark, then the harpoon hits the shark, and the shark sinks out of view. If the harpoon misses, then a 'splash' occurs on the screen to mark the spot, and the players can try again, using the splash mark as feedback."[12]

The model is a representation of shark hunting in a two-dimensional model of ocean space. The game uses a spatial model to teach estimation skills involved in two-dimensional mapping from position to number. In a simpler version of the game, the shark exists in one-dimensional space and the children need estimate position on only one number line.

Levin has tested this game with ten-year-olds, who find it challenging and motivating. As for learning, results are available only for the simpler, one-dimensional version of the game. Levin reports that within ten games children move from random performance to high accuracy.

The process of learning. Perhaps even more interesting than this rapid learning are the processes, both cognitive and social, that go on as the children move toward proficiency. On the cognitive side, children often start out with their own concept of the task. For example, some children initially acted as though they thought the task was to get the path of the harpoon to *cross* the shark rather than to land on it. Thus, a thematic model (here shark hunting), while it can motivate and aid learning, may also interfere with the main learning objective (here, estimating position on coordinated number lines). At the same time, this type of situation allows children to try out different hypotheses about the nature of the task as defined by the computer program. This process of hypothesis testing is, in itself, a valuable kind of learning.

On the social side, Levin and Kareev observed the following sequence in an after-school computer club: "Initially, a child would work with other children and would also freely use adult help to learn about a new computer program. Next, children would work together without direct adult participation, only drawing in an adult to help when they got blocked in some way. Finally, a child would work either with a friend or alone, gradually making the task more challenging if the program allowed this."[13]

This sequence shows how cooperative activity can benefit learning, and how the computer can foster cooperative enterprise. Such cooperation seems to occur primarily when there are fewer computers than children wanting to use them and the computers have to be shared.[14] Thus, under certain conditions, the popular stereotype of computers as an essentially asocial technology does not apply.

The sequence also illustrates the appeal of challenge. In Harpoon, expert players would make the size of the shark smaller, thus increasing the difficulty of hitting it. As they worked with progressively smaller sharks, they developed increasingly accurate number-estimating skills. Children do not want to keep working at a level they have perfected; they seek a new challenge. Harpoon illustrates how this attraction to new challenges can be used in computer games designed for education, as it is in games designed for entertainment. This ability of the computer to keep pace with the child's emerging skills is one of its main advantages as an educational tool.

Computer simulation. The simple model of Harpoon is not, of course, intended to teach children about shark hunting. Another type of computer model, generally more complex than Harpoon, does teach about a real-life situation or system. This type of model is called a simulation. Atari's *Guide to Computers in Education* provides a good overview of the educational possibilities of computer simulation:

> The impact of different national energy policies on the economy, the survival of a herd of caribou, a scientific laboratory experiment, the economics of a small business, the setting up of a space colony, the ecosystem of a pond—virtually any system can be represented by formulae which . . . represent how all the components of the system interrelate. The simulation then allows the student to alter the condition of one or more components and see the consequences of this alteration on the rest of the system. How will unchecked waste disposal alter water quality and affect life forms in a lake? What treatment methods will most effectively restore water quality; and over what period of time? The computer becomes an infinitely variable experimental laboratory for exploratory learning.[15]

One of the first simulations to be developed for young children was called Lemonade Stand. In this simulation, you, the player, start with supplies for making lemonade (provided by your mother). The program gives you information relevant to consumer demand for lemonade (such as a weather forecast), and you have to decide how much lemonade to make and at what price to sell it. The computer then calculates the profit you would make under those conditions. In later turns, your mother stops providing you with sugar, and your decision making must also take the fluctuating price of sugar into account. The point of Lemonade Stand is to maximize profit.

This simulation builds on a real-world model that is familiar to many young children, the lemonade stand. However, it should enable children to go beyond their everyday knowledge of the model to understand relationships between variables such as cost and profit, supply and demand. The computer simulation enables children too young to comprehend abstract discussions of profit, loss, and so on to learn through *doing* how economic variables operate.

It may be that this concrete, action-oriented knowledge can serve as a foundation for later understanding of the concepts on a more abstract level. Perhaps a program like Lemonade Stand not only lets children begin learning the concepts sooner (not necessarily an advantage) but later allows them to learn them more easily and profoundly, say in a high school or college economics class, for having had the experience of actively manipulating them in a concrete situation. This sequence of learning is still speculative. Research is needed to find out what knowledge children of different ages take away from simulations like Lemonade Stand and whether this knowledge can aid the later learning of the same concepts on an abstract level.

Lemonade Stand builds upon and extends children's everyday experience. Simulations can also build upon and extend topics initiated in school. A nice example of this comes from Gompers Secondary Center in San Diego, where a computer simulation of the migration of the California gray whale, written by the San Diego Department of Education, is used in class after the annual whale-watching field trip. The computer provides another medium in what is already a multimedia experience, combining classroom discussion with actual observation.[16]

What is the value of augmenting observation with computer simulation? This question was systematically explored in a study that looked at the role of computer simulation in teaching high school physics.[17] Experiments were set up that could be done either in the laboratory or on the computer. One group of students did the experiments on the computer only, one group in the laboratory only; the third group combined computer and lab, doing one trial of each experiment in the laboratory as an example, but using the computer to collect data for analysis. The combination of computer and lab was most effective for the largest number of outcome measures: this group was able to reach conclusions more effectively and had the highest exam scores. The computer alone was most effective in teaching how to investigate relationships between laboratory variables. (This is a higher-level version of what should result for younger children engaged in Lemonade Stand.) The laboratory-only group was not superior to the other two groups on any outcome measure. Thus, the computer is no exception to the principle, which I will emphasize in the next chapter, that a multimedia approach to a topic is often the most effective one.

The program that learns.   Programs that learn are unique to the computer medium and derive directly from its programmability. An example of such a program is a game called Animals, which illustrates the possibilities of learning games that put the player rather than the computer in charge. The game is modeled on the old game of twenty questions. The twist is that the computer starts out knowing only two animals and the player has to teach the computer the names and characteristics of other animals he or she wants to introduce into the game. Essentially this game teaches the logic of class relations while at the same time requiring the player to create a logically structured domain of knowledge. The player creates the knowledge that the computer then uses to play the game. Animals exemplifies how, unlike reading, radio, or television, interactive computer technology can give the child the active role so crucial to the learning process.

WORD PROCESSING

This book was written using a word processing program for an Apple II Plus computer. Thus, as Seymour Papert has pointed out, word processing is an adult, even professional use of the computer that is available to children.[18]

Word processing was my first personal involvement with computers. I was impressed by the changes it made in my thought processes and productive ability: I felt that I could write more quickly and more easily; revision became a pleasure rather than a chore. I was sure the effects must be at least as dramatic for children, so I set about looking for people doing research relating to children's use of word processing. As with the whole area of children and computers, there has not yet been much systematic research on what happens when children have access to word processors. Not all the people I talked to in the field agreed that the effects are dramatic, but I found more agreement about positive effects in this area than in any other I researched for this book.

In word processing (also called text editing) you write

at a computer keyboard, much as you would at a typewriter. The difference is that you see your initial product on the video screen rather than on paper. Because the text you create is in the computer's memory, as well as on the screen, you can make changes electronically, without any need for physically erasing or crossing out. You can even "cut and paste" electronically, moving words, paragraphs, or pages from one part of the text to another with a few keystrokes. The cost of error is reduced to insignificance. In order to get "hard copy" (words typed on paper), you hook up the computer to a printer which puts the text stored in memory (and later transferred to cassette tape or disk) into typewritten form. You give electronic commands, via the computer, for the format of the printed page—margins, underlining, and so forth. You can print out a given piece of text in a different format without retyping it, by simply changing the format commands. Similarly, you can revise the text without retyping, by merely going back to the original version, saved on tape or disk, and electronically revising it.

My first concrete evidence relating to children and word processors came from Jan Austin, an elementary school teacher in northern California. She had given her third and fourth graders the project of writing a book about Native Americans on the computer. The class successfully wrote the book, which they then distributed to other people. This by itself was notable, for it was a much larger writing project than the class had undertaken before. Even more important, it was the best writing the class had done all year. It had depth—because, as Austin eloquently put it, "the children were released from their scribal labor."

One important reason for the improvement in the quality of the children's writing was their willingness and even eagerness to revise, made possible by the ease of electronic revision on the computer. The children revised the text of their book many times. They also got interested in spelling, and in experimenting with print formats. They tried many different formats, and the teacher finally had to insist that they stop experimenting and produce the final product. Even then the children complained that if she had given them just one more day they could have produced a much better book. And these were children who, before the computer, had to be begged to make even the most minor revisions.

The computer also encouraged cooperation among children in the writing project. According to their teacher, this class had had some trouble getting along with one another, but the computer drew them together. There were always three or four children standing around the computer working together on the book. This theme that computers foster cooperation is one that we have met before. But when each child has a computer to write with, they become so involved in writing itself that this sort of cooperative activity does not take place.[19] It seems to be the need to share computers that prompts children to work together.

One way computers can, under the right circumstances, foster cooperative intellectual work is apparent in word processing. The screen makes an individual's thought processes public, open to others who can also observe the screen. It makes writing into an easily observable physical object, which can be manipulated in various ways by other people. Thus, the computer makes the private activity of writing into a potentially public and social one.

It may be that group writing, with its stimulus of other children's points of view, is also necessary for word processing to lead fairly quickly to extensive revision. Researchers at Bank Street College of Education in New York found that eighth graders who used word processors for individual compositions tended to treat the computer like an electronic pencil and paper: they spent time planning their writing in advance and did not do much revision. Nevertheless, even here the children reported doing more spontaneous revision than they normally did without a word processor. Perhaps more important, in the long run, than spontaneous revision is the fact that, when students have access to a word processor, the teacher may *ask* for more revision.[20]

Another interesting point that emerged from the work at Bank Street was the usefulness of word processing for a child with behavior problems. This child had been introduced to word processing in a course and enjoyed it so much that she pursued it after the course was over. In other settings, learning-disabled students have improved their writing skills markedly when given the chance to write on a computer.[21]

High school students seem to be as enthusiastic about word processing as younger children. (Indeed, according to Midian Kurland, children love word processing so much that even lack of typing skill does not deter them.) Julie McGee, director of computer curriculum development at Lyons Township High School in Illinois, reports that students are fascinated by the word processor and are motivated to learn how to use it.[22] Because the computer makes writing less painful, they *want* to write. They are more willing to revise and to correct their mistakes. McGee has also found the word processor useful for group work: her students are using it to produce their yearbook. Like younger children, they enjoy having a typed product, and they help each other with work.

I have had every one of these reactions to writing with a computer, and it would surprise me very much if they did not also apply to other adults. Indeed, professional writers have been attracted to word processing in droves.

In July 1982 the *Los Angeles Times* ran an article about a center to which people can go to rent extremely powerful word processing equipment at an hourly rate. The headline was "A Word-Processing Romance: Center Provides Hourly Rental to Infatuated Users." One customer, Philip Friedman, a successful screenwriter, said,

> I do things here I wouldn't otherwise do . . . You can move stuff around very easily. You can make all kinds of small changes which would require retyping an entire manuscript. You get to create a very visual effect and that's very important. All of this becomes fine tunable in a way that would be impossible unless one is willing to employ a whole platoon of typists. It allows a loosening up for me. It makes me more willing to try different things. It allows me to be more confident and feel like it's going to turn out all right.[23]

Although data are not available to make a direct comparison, the basic effects of word processing seem to be parallel in many respects in children and adults.

Most of the projects with young people mentioned so far are in the midst of controlled studies to assess the effects of word processing on writing, but results are not yet in. One such project, however, has already obtained some important findings. James Levin and his colleagues compared two classes of third and fourth graders: one class had spent four months working with a special word processing program designed for children; the other had had only the writing experience that normally takes place in school. At the beginning and again at the end of the four months, each class was given a topic to write about (with pencil and paper, not a word processor) in a restricted time period. The "before" and "after" writing samples were analyzed for length (number of words) and for overall quality (with an emphasis on adherence to topic and organization).

The researchers found an increase of 64 percent in the number of words in the essays of the class that had worked with the computer; the essays of the other class showed no increase. In addition to quantity, the results also showed a gain in quality as a result of the computer: on a five-point scale of quality, the class exposed to word processing increased from an average score of 2.00 to 3.09, while the other class showed no change in quality ratings.[24] (We do not know to what extent these results were caused by more writing practice in the class with the word processor, and to what extent they were caused simply by using the word processor. However, since the availability of a word processor causes students to spend more time writing, either way the results constitute an effect of word processing.)

These findings, in fact, probably underestimate the effect of the computer, for they are based on writing *without* a computer. I would think that the effect would be stronger if the children trained on the computer were assessed writing on the computer. The comparison used in the study is fairer to the children who were not given computers to use, but it does not reveal the actual power of the computer as a writing tool. I have had the subjective experience reflecting the findings of this study. After writing on my computer for a while, I seemed to be able to compose on a conventional typewriter better than before. But I could write much less fluently and revise less easily on the typewriter than on the word processor itself. The power of a tool can be seen most clearly in the work accomplished with it, not in work done without it.

Levin and his colleagues also studied the cooperative process around word processing in detail. They had children work together in pairs and found great benefit from doing so: "Often when one child encounters a block in writing, the other child, bringing a different point of view, can solve the problem by suggesting an alternative approach. The first child not only benefits from having the immediate problem solved, but is exposed to alternative ways to think about the task."[25] Working in pairs also greatly reduced demands upon the teacher's time. Most of the problems that arose for one student could almost immediately be handled by the other, so the teacher did not have to step in. This freed the teacher to use his time in providing support tailored to the students' individual needs.

This study demonstrates that the computer and the cooperation it elicits allow the teacher to individualize instruction more than conventional methods do, adapting tasks to the needs and skills of different children. As a student gains more experience, the teacher's help can be progressively reduced, thus providing a system of "dynamic support," help that changes as the learner's needs change. The computer itself can also provide individualized and changing help, in the form of more or less structured writing tasks. For example, novice writers were given fill-in-the-blank stories to work on, intermediates were assigned unfinished stories to complete, and advanced writers could start from scratch. This individualization of teaching is a powerful factor in the value of computers for learning.

Seymour Papert, in his book *Mindstorms*, points out why word processors can make children so much more enthusiastic about writing:

> For me, writing means making a rough draft and refining it over a considerable period of time. My image of myself as a writer includes the expectation of an 'unacceptable' first draft that will develop with successive editing into presentable form. But I would not be able to afford this image if I were a third-grader. The physical act of writing would be slow and laborious. I would have no secretary. For most children rewriting a text is so laborious that

the first draft is the final copy, and the skill of rereading with a critical eye is never acquired. This changes dramatically when children have access to computers capable of manipulating text. The first draft is composed at the keyboard. Corrections are made easily. The current copy is always neat and tidy. I have seen a child move from total rejection of writing to an intense involvement (accompanied by rapid improvement of quality) within a few weeks of beginning to write with a computer. Even more dramatic changes are seen when the child has physical handicaps that make writing by hand more than usually difficult or even impossible.[26]

Word processing and thinking. Far more speculative than the effects of word processing on writing are its effects on thinking. In 1969, Sylvia Scribner wrote a provocative paper about the cognitive effects of literacy, in which she argued that literacy is a necessary factor in the development of Piaget's highest stage of cognitive development, the stage of formal operations.[27] One way formal operations are distinguished from the earlier stage of concrete operations is by the ability to rearrange propositions or statements mentally. At the earlier stage, children can mentally rearrange concrete objects, but not abstract statements. For readers unfamiliar with Piaget's theory, figure 8 shows the same problem presented at both a concrete and a formal operational level.

This hypothesis about the effect of literacy on formal operations goes back to a key idea of Piaget's: that cognitive development is a product of the child's active manipulation of the world. This is clearly possible for concrete operations, where the child can manipulate concrete objects. But how could it apply to the abstract skills that are the essence of formal operations? Scribner's answer was writing, a process in which propositions or statements are given an external form, which then allows them to be rearranged in the process of

CONCRETE OPERATIONAL PROBLEM

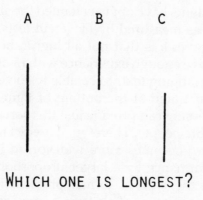

WHICH ONE IS LONGEST?

FORMAL OPERATIONAL PROBLEM

EDITH IS SHORTER THAN LILY
EDITH IS TALLER THAN ANN

WHICH ONE IS TALLEST?

8. *A seriation problem at two levels of cognitive development.*

revision. She noted that formal operations have never been observed in nonliterate cultures. She also cited some data indicating that they do not occur in people with less than a high school education. Yet clearly basic literacy and even a high school education are not sufficient, because a substantial proportion of American college students have not yet attained the stage of formal operations as measured by Piagetian tests.

My hypothesis is that not all high school or college students have enough experience with revision, the process of rearranging text, to be able to solve problems of the sort illustrated at the bottom of figure 8. I believe word processing can provide just this sort of experience to many more people. Therefore, I predict that as writing by computer becomes more widespread it will lead to better performance by a larger proportion of the population on the type of formal problem involving the mental manipulation of abstract propositions.

Composing on the word processor is not enough in itself to lead to formal thinking; practice in revision is necessary. Even in eighth grade, only a small minority of children actively rearrange text when taught to use a word processor. Revision may be more frequent at older ages and in groups. Once word processing equipment becomes more widely available, teachers will be able to encourage students to do more revising. My hypothesis about the effect of word processing on formal operations applies only when the word processor is in fact used to rearrange text in the editing or revision process.

Cognitive requirements for word processing. As mentioned earlier, the basic mechanics of word processing are very easy for children. A study of adults sheds some light on what skills children may possess that make word processing easy: the ability of adults to learn to use a word processor was found to be related primarily to their spatial memory and secondarily to their age.

The better a person's spatial memory (for arrangements of objects), the easier it was for the person to learn to use the word processor. Similarly, the younger the person, the easier it was to learn.

Recall from earlier chapters that children gain spatial skills by watching television. The importance of spatial memory for word processing gives a clue that the skills picked up from television may facilitate working with word processors in particular and computers in general. Although this was a study of adults, the age factor does hint that children may have an advantage over adults in learning to use computer technology, whether this advantage derives from their greater flexibility or their experience with television.

In word processing the medium of print is placed in the context of a new medium, computers. As print decreased in importance relative to the electronic media, writing skills are said to have declined. It will be interesting to see, as computers become more widely available, if the word processor, with all the freedom it gives a writer, will reverse this trend.

PROGRAMMING

Some of the most optimistic thinking about the educational potential of computers focuses on computer programming.

In France, an official government policy report labeled computer programming a "crossroads discipline" comparable in importance to mastery of one's native language and of mathematics. It was proposed that computer science become a compulsory subject in secondary school, with 200 hours of instruction distributed over 4 years. Many educators and parents in this country might endorse such a proposal. The reasons given go beyond the pragmatic employment value of computer skills. As it was once popular to think about the learning of classical languages, computer programming is often considered to be a source of mental discipline that has widespread cognitive consequences. It compels the orderly and precise description of the actions that are required to attain a desired goal; for computers lack the inferential comprehension skills that permit vagueness to succeed in everyday human communication.[30]

As Papert puts it, he wants to see the child program the computer, rather than the computer program the child. And some children do take to programming with enthusiasm. Early reports in the popular press sensationalized child programmers. For example, *Money* magazine ran an article in 1982 about adolescents earning good livings as part-time programmers and software designers. The youngest children featured in the article were two 12-year-old boys who designed a record-keeping program and then set up a company to market it.[31] However, while most children show themselves capable of learning to program simple commands, observations in the Bank Street School indicate that only about 25 percent of all third- and sixth-grade children are highly interested in learning to program. Another quarter are quite uninterested and learn very little. (These results relate to one particular computer language, LOGO. While no research on this yet exists, Sherman Rosenfeld has pointed out that the unstructured aspect of BASIC may be easier than LOGO for young children whose cognitive development does not yet enable them to deal with certain complex logical structures.)

When children do complex programming, video games are their favorite subject.[32] Thus, the games have an important benefit in addition to those mentioned in the previous chapter: they provide motivation for learning programming. Beyond motivation, experience in playing the games should furnish sensorimotor knowledge of what to program. Programming games is a good first step in the symbolic conceptualization and manipulation of complex systems. Because more abstract skills build on practical, sensorimotor experience, video games can furnish a solid foundation for the symbolic representation of complex, interactive, dynamic systems.

A computer program is basically a systematic set of instructions for the computer. The instructions must be written in a special language that the computer understands. LOGO is one such language, designed especially to introduce children to programming. It was developed by Papert and his colleagues at MIT. Because the computer cannot make inferences, the instructions must be completely explicit. As a ten-year-old at the Bank Street School said about the computer: "It's dumb. I have to tell it everything."

This quality has an important positive side as well. One potential effect of the computer's need for explicitness is to make procedural details that are implicitly taken for granted in everyday life explicit and therefore conscious. Papert gives a nice example of this from turtle geometry, a system for learning geometry by programming the visible path of an entity, called a turtle, using the LOGO language. Say a child wants to program his turtle (visible on the computer screen as a triangle of light) to make a circle. The child is first asked to "play turtle," to move his body the way the turtle must move to make a circle. This might lead to a description such as "When you walk in a circle you take a little step forward and you turn a little. And you keep doing it." The next step is to express this description in programming language: TO CIRCLE REPEAT (FORWARD 1 RIGHT 1).[33] This program or set of instructions tells the computer to move the triangle one unit ahead, one to the side, and keep repeating this sequence. The child who gets to this point has become conscious in a new way of what it means to walk in a circle. Such awareness is necessary for the child to program the computer, although it was not necessary for the child to program him or herself to walk.

A careful study of children and teachers using LOGO indicate that the steps in such a sequence do not happen spontaneously. There is need for a more structured instructional context than Papert advocates.[34] As with print, exposure to the medium itself is not enough for particular skills to develop; just as children have to be taught to read, they need instruction in programming computers.

Papert's example can be used to illustrate another important point. This program for generating a circle is based on differential geometry, a type of geometry that is part of differential calculus. It contrasts, for example, with a computer program based on Euclidean geometry, where the circle is defined in terms of a constant distance of all points from the center. Euclidean geometry is usually taught several years before differential calculus. The computer makes possible an inversion of the order of learning the two geometries. Papert believes that computer programming may make what have been considered very advanced cognitive skills possible at much younger ages. While claims such as these are provocative and have generated much interest, there is as yet little relevant scientific evidence.

Effects of programming. The same study of classes using LOGO found that pupils gained in general computer literacy from a year of experience with LOGO. They knew more about the uses of computers, for example, and they understood that a computer needs very literal and explicit instructions. They could also discuss the relative advantages and disadvantages of two different computers for different programming functions. This kind of knowledge will be useful for adults in the future, who will come into frequent contact with computers, whether or not they program them themselves.

Is there any hard evidence that what children learn from programming transfers to other cognitive skills? Such evidence would be required to substantiate the claims made in the French government's policy report. There is some evidence that computer programming can help children learn mathematics. For example, learning to write programs to generate and print number series helped eleven-year-olds to solve problems involving the mathematical concept of a variable.[35]

LOGO programming has also been used to impart physics concepts. Andrea DiSessa and Papert taught physics in the MIT Artificial Intelligence Laboratory using a modified version of the turtle, called the "dynaturtle." The dynaturtle looks like the turtle used in geometry, but its movement follows the laws of physics rather than those of mathematics.

> In the dynaturtle environment, students control the motion of the turtle by 'pushing' it with forces of specified direction and magnitude. The turtle then moves on the screen according to the laws of Newtonian physics as if it were an object on a frictionless surface.
>
> One of the first surprises students have in this environment is that the turtle doesn't always move in the direction they push it. For example, if the turtle is moving upward and the student wants it to change direction and go sideways, he cannot just give it a sideways push. Instead, he must give it a push with a direction and magnitude that completely counteract the upward motion and also impart a sideways motion.[36]

Figure 9 illustrates the difference between the way a student might expect the dynaturtle to move and the way it actually does move when given a sideways push.

The dynaturtle can be used to impart an intuitive understanding of elementary mechanics that is very hard to get in traditional learning environments. One reason is that frictionless surfaces are not generally available. The relative ineffectiveness of the more usual methods of teaching physics for transmitting this set of concepts is demonstrated by the fact that MIT physics students who played with the dynaturtle did almost as poorly as elementary school students.[37]

There is only one real piece of evidence of transfer from programming to a general cognitive skill that has no direct connection to the programming: after a year of LOGO, nine- to eleven-year-old children did better on a word puzzle and a permutation task than a comparison group without programming experience.[38] The permutation task (in which the child is asked to rearrange a set of elements in as many ways as possible) has special significance because permutations and combinations are part of formal operational thinking. For this reason, it constitutes a piece of support for Papert's claim that, by making the abstract concrete, programming will develop formal operational skills.

Programming and social interaction. The world of turtles and dynaturtles may sound like a solitary and mech-

MOVES UPWARD   PUSH SIDEWAYS   ACTUAL MOVEMENT
                     AND EXPECTED MOVEMENT

9. *An error in a student's conception of motion. (Adapted from DiSessa, "LOGO Project, Massachusetts Institute of Technology.")*

anistic one, without human contact, in which individual students sit alone and stare at video screens. Many people seem to think of computers in this way. To investigate the impact of computer programming on children's social contacts and interaction, Bank Street researchers observed children aged eight to eleven in classrooms where they were learning to program in LOGO. The researchers observed the children both when they were working with computers and when they were engaged in the more traditional classroom activities. (The opportunity for interaction was available in both types of situation because all observations were made in work periods, which were not directed by the teacher.) The children collaborated more with each other, both verbally and nonverbally, when they worked with computers than when they engaged in other activities.[39] The surprising sociability of computer activity, at least in the classroom, is a theme that has come up over and over in my research for this book. It seems that the common fears about the dehumanizing or mechanizing influence of the computer may be at least partially unfounded and that the computer's effect in the classroom may generally be quite the opposite.

LOOKING TO THE FUTURE

In the words of O. K. Tikhomirov, "Just as the development of gasoline engines provided a tool for human physical activity, so the development of the computer provided a tool for human mental activity . . . Tools are not just added to human activity; they transform it."[40] Will the computer, as Tikhomirov claims, truly transform mental activity? In the one area where computers are most fully functioning in the capacity of a tool— word processing—they do seem to be transforming the child's (and the adult's) relationship to writing. Perhaps when all is said and done, the computer's biggest contribution to education will turn out to be a motivational one: computers capture the interest of students who would normally be dropouts from the educational system. At Garfield High School, in the middle of the Latino barrio of Los Angeles, the rate of absenteeism for computer classes is less than 5 percent, compared with 20 percent for the school overall. Students not only come to class, they also stay after school and come back on Saturdays to do computer work. An important tribute to the motivational power of the computer comes from a student, Margarita Vargas: "Students are more interested in working on computers right now than in spending time on the streets."[41]

9 / Multimedia Education

Many threads in this book lead up to the idea that we should incorporate the electronic media into education, expanding beyond the current orientation of schools toward print and oral language. First, each medium has its own strengths and weaknesses, and each emphasizes certain types of information, ways of thinking, and modes of perception. Thus, we need multimedia education as a way of developing all facets of the mind and teaching children to be open to different perspectives.

Second, the educational impact of a medium is enhanced when it becomes the subject of dialogue and discussion. School is the setting where such discussion can most easily take place. Print is now the most frequent object of classroom discussion; this adds greatly to its value as an educational tool. The other media could benefit as well. The other side of this coin is the school's potential for influencing the child's perception of and response to different media. As discussed earlier, curricula organized around television can give children a more sophisticated and critical approach to viewing. We already take this for granted with literature.

Third, a multimedia approach to a subject can be a more effective way of teaching than a single medium in isolation. I gave an instance of this in Chapter 8: high school physics students learned more from a combination of laboratory work with computer-simulated experiments than from either technique alone.

Fourth, as seen in Chapter 5, the electronic media can be used to make education and even literacy more widely accessible, raising the educational level of whole groups and populations. From this point of view, multimedia education is a way of making education more democratic: it cannot eliminate differences among groups, but it can bring more people into the educational process and raise the average level of knowledge and skill.

GUIDING HOME VIEWING

Teachers can have a strong influence on what children watch in their homes. In the research on *Freestyle,* a program designed to counter sex and ethnic stereotypes about careers, teachers reminded one group of students to watch the show at home. This teacher guidance produced a rate of home viewing almost seven times higher than the national norm for the program.[1] This higher rate of viewing increased learning from the show, because, as is often the case, learning was proportional to exposure. Thus, teachers can influence both which programs children watch and how much they learn from them.

One of my children's junior high school teachers, Rick Takagaki, for a time prepared a weekly list of worthwhile shows for students to watch. The list, which ranged from old movies to talk shows, included far more challenging shows than those my children normally watched. They did occasionally watch programs from the list, sometimes writing an extra-credit paper on one (a problem was that the viewing was an optional part of the course, which was social studies). One thing that struck me about the lists was that I, as a television-illiterate parent, could not possibly have created such a list, even if I had the time to try.

The *Freestyle* research indicates that children's viewing can be quite affected by suggestions from teachers. Takagaki's approach indicates the potential influence on children's viewing a thoughtful and television-literate teacher can have. Even wider possibilities might open up if such a list were made a central, required part of a course and if viewing were combined with classroom discussion.

Indeed, the school may be the *only* practical way to influence the way children watch TV and what they watch. Comparing school and home as sources of guidance for children's television viewing, Dorothy and Jerome Singer found that it was easier to influence what children watch on TV and how they watch it by working through the schools than by working through parents.[2] I can think of a number of reasons why it would be difficult to work through parents. Most parents work, and this is probably all the more true for the parents of children who watch large quantities of television. Parents who work and tend to need television as an electronic babysitter are just those who probably lack the time and energy to educate their children about television. In general, parents are at a disadvantage relative to teachers in the time, energy, and knowledge necessary to guide their children's TV watching.

This is certainly not to discourage parents from guiding their children's viewing. They should do all they possibly can. It is to say that their task can be very much helped by the schools. Parents are generally in a better position to know what they do *not* want their children to watch than what they do. It is in making positive suggestions that the school can be most important.

TELEVISION IN THE SCHOOL

We have seen that making a television show the focus of interaction with an adult enhances children's learning from that show. One reason for this is that such interaction makes children realize that mental effort is expected of them. Children tend to approach television as an "easy" medium, expend little mental effort on watching it, and therefore learn rather superficially from it.[3] In contrast, they view print as more difficult, invest more mental effort, and learn more deeply from it. However, if children are told to look carefully and try to learn from television, the depth of learning becomes greater: television viewing comes to resemble reading in this respect. If television were part of school assignments, teachers would very naturally give just this type of instructional message.

Studying television. Television is treated as a serious object of study in an elementary school curriculum designed by Rosemary Lehman that takes as its subject the formal features of television, the medium's code and aesthetics.[4] This curriculum takes the code that constitutes television literacy (see Chapter 2) and turns it into an object of study. As a class in English literature might talk about the techniques and style of Shakespeare and Dickens, children in Lehman's program talk about the techniques and style of television programs.

Lehman's curriculum is divided into different areas of television technique, such as light and shadow, color, forms, motion, and time/space. For example, in the area of motion, children learn to distinguish camera movement from person movement and to find times when both camera and person move together. In the area of time/space, they discuss the differences among objective time (clock time of the program), the illusion of time created by editing, and subjective time (whether time moves quickly or slowly for the viewer). Whereas the techniques of print literature, based on verbal forms, are difficult for younger children to perceive and analyze, the forms of television make use of children's well-developed visual abilities: abilities which, as we have seen, television both exploits and fosters.

Lehman's curriculum was tested for a school year with eight- and nine-year-old children. These children were compared at the end of the year with another class taught by the same teacher without the television curriculum. In writing about a short television sequence, the children who had studied the forms and aesthetics of television commented on formal features such as color and composition; children in the other group wrote only about story line. Children in the first group were also much more able to think of questions they could ask themselves while watching television; they used more cues of shadow, perspective, simulated motion, and so forth in drawing a scene from a TV program; and they were better able to indicate sound to go with their picture.

The year of studying television also caused a shift in the children's television-viewing tastes: action and formula programs dropped from their lists of favorite shows and were replaced by more challenging programs. No such change took place in the other class. For example, among the children who had studied television, *Charlie's Angels* dropped from first to tenth place; it was replaced by the evening movies. Whereas no documentaries or docudramas were on the list of favorites before the course, *Holocaust* appeared in the top ten afterwards.

These results are important. They show that elementary school children can analyze the forms of television, much as we might expect older children to analyze the forms of literature. In so doing, children take a more active approach to the medium, becoming aware not only of content but of how television's forms and techniques create that content. In short, they become aware of the message of their medium.

Equally important, treating television as a serious object of study makes children expend more effort in viewing television, so that they choose more challenging programs. If this type of television course could be widely taught in the schools, the level of popular taste might increase greatly and there might therefore be a public demand for higher-quality programming. This could have a tremendous impact on television in the United States, where audience ratings determine a program's fate on the commercial networks.

Note that this type of course does not depend upon the overall quality of program content that is available. It depends only on having a range of techniques on the air. Thus, it is a positive approach to television, and one that can make use of formula comedies, commercials, and action shows, as well as of more "educational" programming.

Critical skills. Another approach to teaching about television in the schools focuses on turning children into critical viewers. I mentioned such efforts in the area of commercials and the nature of television reality in Chapter 4. These curricula aim to counteract the bad effects of U.S. commercial television, rather than to use television in a constructive way. Camera techniques tend to be treated as devices for deception rather than for art. In fact, of course, the techniques have both sides to them. This type of curriculum does, however, contribute to children's awareness of the medium. Both approaches to the study of television have distinctive contributions to make, and children would benefit from being exposed to both approaches in elementary school.

It would also be useful to bring feature films into the schools as objects of study and analysis. Just as with television, both an aesthetic and a critical approach to film could be developed in the classroom. In the United States certain feature films, such as *Star Wars*, are seen almost universally by children. Recall from Chapter 4 that seeing a film once can have a profound effect on social attitudes. Yet as of now the powerful images of film are assimilated by children automatically without any of the criticism, information, or analysis that would enable them to make choices about how to incorporate what they have seen into their own attitudes.

TELEVISION IN THE SERVICE OF PRINT

Many parents and teachers might worry that spending so much time on television in the classroom could further erode reading and writing skills. However, the electronic media can also be used in schools to help build print literacy. In Chapter 8, I discussed the positive effect of word processing on writing skills; Chapter 5 showed how schools have used *The Electric Company* to build basic reading skills.

Television and film can also be used to enhance the comprehension and enjoyment of literature, especially on the part of the less able students. Working with junior high school students, Elias Levinson looked at how their response to short stories (by authors such as O. Henry) differed depending on the medium of presentation. One group of students read the original story; another group both read the story and saw it on film. Levinson investigated their comprehension (including recall) and enjoyment (assessed by the desire to read more stories of the same type). Overall, he found that the addition of the film very much increased comprehension and enjoyment, especially for students with lower IQ's. The advantage added by the film was also greater for the more unfamiliar stories, indicating that film or television could be particularly valuable for unfamiliar subjects or genres.[5]

It is interesting that the films stimulated not only comprehension and memory of the story but also a desire to read more similar stories. It is also important that the effect of film on reading is greatest for the children who tend to have more problems in school, that is, the low-IQ group. This study demonstrates the potential for using television to enhance reading. Contrary to popular opinion, books and television need not be two media at war with each other.

Indeed, movies tend to make certain books popular with children. A survey of sixth, seventh, and eighth graders in New Jersey showed that 40 percent of the books they chose to read were tied to television or movies. In England in the 1950s it was found that both television and radio dramatizations, some serialized, caused many children to read the dramatized books, many of which were classics.[6]

Some teachers are beginning to take advantage of television's ability to motivate reading. A flavor of the rather dramatic results that can be obtained is conveyed by Rosemary Lee Potter, a pioneer in the use of out-of-school television in school:

> One day a sixth-grader named Clara came in with a paperback copy of *The Little House on the Prairie*. Clara was not a great reader. I had never seen her with an unassigned book. It was quite a surprise for me to see her bring in a rather thickish book and read it. No doubt noticing my surprise, she quickly explained to me that *she had seen it on TV!* . . . I scoured book shelves, libraries, and booklists . . . I found a bounty of television-related books for my students . . . I began to bring these books into the classroom. Students showed high interest. Most of the books soon fell apart with excessive wear. Students who had previously been nonreaders

read everything from the latest about Fonzie to well-known books like *Sounder*.[7]

Another way of using television in the schools, one that has become increasingly common in the United States in recent years, is to read television scripts in the classroom. The television networks now release their scripts in advance; CBS distributes millions of scripts and coordinated teacher's guides each year. There is an organization, Capital Cities Television Reading Program, that distributes advance scripts, along with co-ordinated teacher's guides and student workbooks. Teachers in Philadelphia who used scripts from television programs reported improved reading scores and much more interest in reading. Scripts were even stolen from the classroom, the first known theft of reading material in that school.[8]

Television shows and films can also be treated as literature in school. Sharon Neuwirth, a fourth grade teacher, noticed that her children were retelling their favorite television shows in class in great detail, but that they were totally oblivious to the story line. (Her observation agrees with the experimental research on the subject.)[9] She noticed the same tendency to focus on peripheral detail in discussing stories read in class and in book reports. To counteract this, Neuwirth developed a project to teach story comprehension, focusing on conflict as the key to a story's structure:

I explained to the students that a conflict is set up when a character has a problem to solve: he wants or needs something, but an obstacle stands in his way. For example, a new student wants to make friends, but he's shy. Or a teacher is determined to help a student who wants to drop out of school . . .

To tune the students into looking for the basic conflict, I gave them an unusual homework assignment: watch anything you like on TV, and be prepared tomorrow to tell about your show in only three sentences—Who the show was about, what the main character wanted, and what stood in his or her way.[10]

From this assignment, Neuwirth had the class branch off into identifying conflict in other media: film, school plays, and short stories. One effect of learning to understand the basic structure of a story was that the children could, for the first time, read long novels. They had been unable to do so before because, lacking a sense of overall structure, they were simply overwhelmed by complex plots.

Neuwirth's project succeeded because she began with television. The medium was available to all the children, no matter what their reading level, and they were already highly motivated to watch and discuss television shows. Once concepts were learned in relation to this familiar medium, they could be transferred to more difficult and less familiar ones, notably print. Surely this program will make children more sophisticated and comprehending viewers, as well as making them better readers.

One reason why the transfer of skills from television to print works so well may be that children start at a higher level of expertise in the former medium. In England, Michael Scarborough has investigated the educational use of entertainment television with ten and eleven-year-old children, and has come to the following conclusions:

> Perhaps the most significant outcome to emerge from this effort was the considerable depth and sophistication in the child's conceptualisation. Certainly they more readily articulated their understanding of programmes than they might have done had the exercise been based on written material of comparable content and difficulty.

It might be that this is an indication of the child's intelligence and scholastic achievement, from my work it is impossible to say clearly if this is so, but my opinion is that because there is a widespread familiarity with the medium of television, children of a wide range of abilities are at ease in expressing their understanding of what they have viewed.[11]

THE CASE FOR MULTIMEDIA EDUCATION

These classroom techniques could all be interpreted as showing the value of multimedia education: in each case, television or film is an addition to print, not a substitute for it. Indeed, one of the most consistent findings in the literature on media in education is the superiority of multimedia over single-medium presentation.[12] In fact, in talking about media in schools, one is always talking about adding media to the original medium of face-to-face interaction with the teacher. And face-to-face interaction adds as much to the learning value of any medium as the medium adds to the classroom.

There are various reasons why it should be of value to have the same material presented through more than one medium. Each medium, because of its code of representation and its technical capabilities, must emphasize different kinds of information. For example, film or television emphasizes action and simultaneous events happening in parallel. Print, in contrast, emphasizes a linear, sequential relationship between ideas or events. Thus, to receive information on the same topic through different media is to learn about the topic from different points of view.[13]

Our present educational system is so print-oriented that we tend to think of an account in print as the "true" one. In education, print is truly a privileged medium of communication. This is probably mainly a result of historical circumstance: print was there first. It is time to question this assumption, not thinking of replacing print, but of moving from domination by a single medium to an increasingly multimedia system.

Examples of multimedia education. In England important steps have been taken to incorporate television into schooling. An extensive system of school broadcasts, presented cooperatively by the BBC (public) and the ITV (private), includes series on a wide variety of subjects at every level of education from preschool through university. Teacher's booklets for each series provide ideas for preparation before a broadcast and follow-up afterwards. While these broadcasts are not perfectly integrated into the curriculum, they are very broadly used and widely accepted by teachers.

In Sweden, careful thought has been given to how best to combine media in schools. Rolf Lundgren, director of the instructional programming unit of the Swedish Broadcasting Corporation, gives an example of the complementary strengths of television and print in a multimedia package:

> If it is a question of giving students facts and people, let the printed material give them the facts, and television the people. Suppose we want to give the students an idea of what the Swedish society does to take care of its alcoholics. Information on how many alcoholics there are, where in the country there are special clinics for them, how much they cost the taxpayers, etc., all those kinds of facts could be better given in printed form than in a program. In the program we could follow an alcoholic's normal day, thus giving the student a moving document of the seamy side of the welfare state. Let the printed material take care of the cognitive aspects and the program of the emotional aspects of the matter . . . In the example mentioned—which is part of a

multi-media project we produced a couple of years ago—
the TV program gave the students the case of an unfortunate fellowman and they could not help being affected by what they saw; in the classroom discussions
that followed they could generalize their program
impressions with the help of the factual information given
them in the pupil's pamphlet.[14]

Another Swedish technique was to use radio to give
commentary on the case viewed in the film, presenting,
for example, interviews with social workers and other
people who come into contact with alcoholics. Radio is
also used for purely verbal or aural material, including
drill concerning material presented on television.

As we saw in Chapter 4, one of television's strengths
is in conveying feelings. Print, in contrast, is good for
facts. Finally, discussion not only provides the active
element so essential for learning; it also helps transform
the specifics observed on television into generalizations.
I have the feeling that one limitation of television is its
tendency to use concrete examples, easily shown in visual images, and to avoid generalizations. Print and discussion, however, lend themselves well to abstract
generalization, precisely because they can be divorced
from concrete images. Combining television with these
other media can turn television's weakness into a strength,
as it provides the concrete examples that make abstract
generalizations meaningful.

In my experience teaching developmental psychology
to university undergraduates, I have also found the various media to be complementary. I use audio recordings
to present experiments that are primarily verbal in nature. I use film and video to show children's behavior
and reactions at different ages and to show environ-
mental settings that would not otherwise be accessible
to most students. For example, it is virtually impossible
to describe infant reflexes in a way that is meaning-

ful to someone who has never seen one. Film lets the students see it. Through film, my students are able to observe infant care on an Israeli kibbutz or to meet a family that has lost a child to Tay-Sachs disease.

Film can get students emotionally involved with the material, and I take advantage of that, using film as a basis for group discussion. But the lazy habits born of too much entertainment television can cause students to consider the films as breaks in the class, opportunities to "space out." It is necessary to establish a context for their active involvement with the film material. I do this primarily by telling the students that the films are integral to the course and they will be tested on them. I also introduce each film, embedding it thoroughly in the structure of the class—a technique that has been shown to enhance learning from a film. An informal survey in my classroom confirmed an experimental finding mentioned earlier: a film image makes a point from lecture or reading more memorable.

After showing a film, I use lecture to relate the concrete examples presented in film to general facts and theories. For example, following the film of the Tay-Sachs family, I might talk about the frequency and genetic mechanism of Tay-Sachs disease; after a film showing infant care on a kibbutz, I would talk about how infants who have been raised on a kibbutz tend to turn out. I also use textbooks, which have strengths similar to those of lectures but can cover a still larger range of fact and theory. Textbooks often provide general background and factual tie-ins for the films as well. Finally, I have the students observe children in order to test some facts and theories for themselves, to experience the methods from which facts are derived in the field, and to become personally involved in the material.

Thus, each medium—video or film, face-to-face communication, print, and experiment—contributes a unique point of view on a common set of topics. Together they provide memorability, active learning, factual content, and generalizations about the field. While this example is simply based on my personal experience, it agrees with the facts that have been accumulating about each medium and about the value of multimedia learning.

Comparative media studies. If different media present different views on the same subject, then one interesting task which could be carried out in school is to compare these views in a systematic way: comparative media studies. Contrast is a major psychological mechanism for bringing something into awareness. I do not think it a coincidence that our first scientific knowledge of literacy began just when the electronic media became important. Before the advent of the newer media, print was considered a transparent carrier of information. The biases intrinsic to its form could not be imagined so long as it was the only medium of mass communication. When the electronic media revealed themselves as different from print, they furnished a contrasting background that made the qualities of the print medium "visible" for the first time. This idea of contrast can be applied to children's education. Comparative media studies could make children aware of the style, techniques, and biases of each medium.

New combinations of media. The newest electronic media, video games and computers, also have promising applications to education, as Chapters 7 and 8 revealed. Recall that the combination of computer simulations and real laboratory experiments is better than either medium alone for teaching physics. In France, computer simulations have been added to biology courses to enable students to do experiments in areas such as embryological development to which they would not ordinarily have access.[15] Simulation programs could be incorporated into the teaching of subjects from math to the social sciences, yielding multimedia combinations with computers for almost every subject area. Learning software is another application of computers to education, one that is a useful addition to instruction traditionally using other media.

There are a number of areas in which the computer can serve as a tool for another medium, rather than as a learning environment in itself.[16] In word processing (discussed in Chapter 8), the computer is a tool for the print medium. Music is another such area; personal computers allow even novices to experiment with musical composition. In art, programs such as Color Sketch provide an electronic Etch-a-Sketch, in which it is possible to change colors at will, erase, and redraw. Other graphics programs provide more flexibility, even including the possibility of computer animation.

A brand-new development is the use of television and computer together. Samuel Gibbon, Cynthia Char, and their colleagues at the Bank Street College of Education are working on a science program, *The Voyage of the Mimi*, that will combine a television series with computer programs. In this program, two scientists and their teenage assistants study whales on a boat that has a computer on board. Computer programs are being developed for use in schools in conjunction with the television show. For example, one is a simulation of navigation techniques, which involves fairly complex mathematics; another involves graphing data, such as data on water temperature over time; a third uses the theme of a whale search to teach simple commands in the computer language LOGO. This project gives some idea of the combinations of media that will be possible in the education of the future.

As for video games, I have already mentioned that they can motivate children to do computer programming. Another example of the possibilities for video games in multimedia education is provided by Levin and Kareev, using a game called Roadrace. The game has potential learning value in itself: for hand-eye coordination, integrating information (speed and position), attention span, and reading numbers (speed, time, and points earned appear continuously on the screen). Roadrace can also supply motivation and information for other learning activities. In a fourth-grade classroom, Levin and Kareev had children who had played Roadrace for a while go on to keep track of their scores in writing, ultimately teaching them how to do so by plotting graphs. They present other ideas for extending Roadrace into mathematics, such as learning about averages by averaging scores, or learning about the design of experiments by trying to figure out the effects of different race courses.[17]

Multimedia combinations involving video games and computers are just beginning. Knowing what we know about computer technology, computers should have contributions to make to the other media in allowing individualization of instruction, active participation in learning, powerful tools, and experimentation with complex systems.

Videodisc. Videodisc is a new medium that in itself is a multimedia combination. It combines the ability of film or television to present images and sound with the ability of computers to individualize and allow interaction. For example, videodisc can allow the viewer to write his or her own story by presenting alternative choices as a story progresses. Once a choice is made, the outcome is shown on film. This simple example shows how videodisc can make television both more individualized and more participatory. (A videodisc game, Dragon's Lair, was the hit of the summer of 1983 in U.S. video arcades.)

THE NEW VIDEO TECHNOLOGIES

Cable television. Cable television is changing the shape of our media environment in the United States. By multiplying the number of stations available, cable multiplies the choice of materials to use in all the ways I have suggested. By providing at least one network specialized for children's programming, it is greatly increasing the amount of suitable children's programming available.

In addition, some of the more specialized stations provide new kinds of content that could be very useful for instructional purposes. For example, the daily broadcasting of the congressional proceedings could be used in government classes. Recordings from the Spanish-language channels could be used in teaching Spanish as a foreign language. Also, community-access channels make it possible for students' work in video to be broadcast throughout the community, providing a greater motivation for children's television production. Cable broadcasting of student television has already begun to happen.

But all is not rosy with cable television. It is also multiplying the ills of over-the-air television. The violence of police shows has a new and pernicious relative in the "videos" shown continuously on MTV (Music Television) to accompany rock music. These surrealistic videos are generally sadomasochistic, with the rock stars in the leading roles. Because rock musicians are heroes to teenagers, these images are likely to have even more effect on social behavior than the images of a regular television program. Because kids listen to music for hours on end, the existence of MTV will also increase time in front of the television for many pre-adolescents and adolescents.

Cable is still too new for us to know exactly what it will do or what its final shape will be. I mention it mainly to put across the idea that the media environment of children is in a constant state of change and development. Our notions about children and the media need to take this fact into account.

Video recording. The relatively recent availability of new technology for recording television shows and playing them back at will makes it feasible to use broadcast television during regular school hours. This technology overcomes the obstacle of fixed broadcast schedules, which had been a practical barrier to the use of broadcast television in the classroom.[18] For the first time, broadcast television can be fitted to classroom time slots. But the implications of video recording are as much intellectual as practical. With video recordings, a bit of tape can be viewed again or slowed down, for the sort of active analysis that a few lines of poetry or other literature can be subjected to. James Hosney, a teacher teaching film to fourteen- and fifteen-year-olds, told me he could see a large difference in student writing on a film when they had viewed the film twice rather than once. This is something we take for granted in teaching literature.

Whereas playing a whole program or film at once can encourage teachers to be lazy, it is said, "video material used in slices forces the teacher to use it imaginatively and purposefully."[19] Narrated instructional films sometimes do too much for both teacher and student; they present the lecture for the teacher and allow the student no time for reaction. A short piece of unnarrated video recorded by teacher or student can be embedded in the viewers' own structure, allowing more active participation by both student and teacher.

Video recorders make it possible to use television in

many ways that books are now used. Parents can make selective videotape libraries for children's use at home. When school libraries can have video players and collections of videotapes, teachers will be able to assign viewing as they now assign reading for later discussion in class. This is particularly important for film as literature, because feature films are often too long to be shown in class. Also, teachers can make collections of videotapes recorded off the air, as well as with a camera, for repeated use in instruction in various subjects.

Not the least of the uses of the video camera is for teaching sports. Filming people as they engage in a sport is already quite common in some sports, although little has been done with young children in this area. This technique permits the learner to see him or herself from an outsider's perspective, while also making use of television's facility with the portrayal of movement (discussed in Chapter 3).

THE CHILD AS PRODUCER

Recording with a camera also opens the way for the child to act as producer. In the medium of print, children are from the beginning both consumers and producers. They learn to write as well as to read. As computers are being introduced into educational settings, it is becoming increasingly accepted that children will learn how to program as well as to use software. When radio and then television came into existence, however, this producing role was left behind. Until recently, the expense and complexity of the technology put the production of video and audio materials out of the range of the overwhelming majority of children. It is time to rethink the child as producer of these media, because the technologies of production are now much more accessible. Audio recording is within reach of most children in industrial countries, and video recording equipment is becoming increasingly small, cheap, and sophisticated.

Because production always involves more knowledge than does mere perception,[20] it seems likely that once children have had experience as producers they will be more sophisticated consumers. This seems to be true in the domain of computers; knowledge of basic computer programming makes children more knowledgable about computers and their uses. There are other possible benefits of producing as well. Salomon reports on a study by Chava Tidhar in which children planned, shot, and edited eight-millimeter films: "The effects of each of these activities were measured against the mastery of such mental skills as imagery, spatial construction, story completion, and chunking. Filmmaking has profound cognitive effects. But the activity of greatest influence was editing, and the skills most strongly affected were the most general and least TV-specific ones (story completion, story construction, headline generation)."[21] These results indicate great promise for film or video production in terms of general cognitive effects. Furthermore, television production can be exciting, and it is a valuable skill in its own right. No one feels the need to justify teaching children to write because it helps another skill. Why should our attitude toward television or film production be any different?

As for aural media, cassette recording could be widely used right now to give children experience as producers. Children could easily record and edit their own "radio" programs. Both video and audio could be used for documentary as well as artistic purposes. In this role, they would be a valuable adjunct to instruction in all the social sciences. Allowing children to act as producers helps overcome the limitations of the electronic media as relatively passive, one-way forms of communication.

Screenplays. Another way in which children, at least

older children, can take a producing role in the visual media, a way that also involves practice in writing, is by writing screenplays. James Hosney used this technique in a ninth-grade class dealing with both film and literature. The students were asked to take a story they had written earlier in the year and translate it into a screenplay, with accompanying story board. (The storyboard presents a pictorial image of each individual camera shot.) In a very active way this involves the essence of comparative media studies: the translation of one medium into another. Students had to take something that was in words and translate it into visual images, an extremely demanding and involving activity. According to Hosney, the students learned a great deal about the nature of both media from doing this exercise in creative translation.

CONCLUSIONS

Bringing the electronic media into the schools could capitalize on the strong motivational qualities that these media have for children. Many children who are turned off by school are not turned off by one or another of the electronic media; quite the opposite. An educational system that capitalized on this motivation would have a chance of much greater success. I think it would also make education seem more tied to the "real world," where the importance of the electronic media relative to print, is probably the reverse of their relative importance in the world of the school.

Each medium has its own profile of cognitive advantages and disadvantages, and each medium can be used to enhance the impact of the others. In short, to return to Marshall McLuhan, each medium has its own message. The cognitive message of print is the opportunity for reflection. Print and radio share the messages of imagination, articulateness, and serial processing. The messages of television and film are an audiovisual style of communication (similar to that of face-to-face communication) and skill in interpreting the two-dimensional representation of movement and space. It may be that television and video games share the cognitive message of parallel processing. Finally, video games and computers add the message of interactive learning and the experience of complex interacting variables. The computer is such an open-ended and flexible medium that it also shares messages with many of the media that preceded it. It is interactive like face-to-face communication; it can be a carrier for print, as in word-processing; it can be used to program the animated graphics of television or film. It seems too early to say what its final effect on human consciousness will be.

The set of cognitive messages delivered by a particular medium, is, in at least a metaphoric sense, the consciousness created by that medium. It would be a mistake, it seems to me, to become too entrenched in the messages of any one medium. Each cognitive message has its own special value.

Educators (myself included) have a tendency to be literary snobs, regretting the passing of an old order in which people *really* knew how to read and write. This attitude has prevented us from seeing the revolutionary promise of the electronic media: they give new cognitive possibilities to disadvantaged groups, and they have the potential to enrich and diversify educational experience for everyone.

Society is also in direct need of the skills that are developed through experience with the electronic media. Already most people receive most of their information from television, not from print. Feature films provide children's most universal cultural experiences. Thus the need for sophisticated viewing skills is great. Our automobiles are electronic audio environments. Video games are the most lucrative of all the entertainment industries. Computers are inside many items in our everyday environment, and are spreading into homes by leaps and bounds. Most of tomorrow's occupations will involve computers in one form or another, and video games will be most children's first experience in interacting with a computer.

It is not clear how helpful today's television viewing will be for tomorrow's jobs. But society does have a need for people with sophisticated visual skills. E. S. Ferguson, in a 1977 article in *Science,* pointed out that the language of technology is basically nonverbal, and that people involved in technology need to be able to think in terms of images.[22] He said that engineering schools are biased toward educating students to analyze systems using numbers rather than visual images. This bias has produced a lack of people who have the skills to deal with the complexities of real machines and materials.

This bias toward the type of symbol systems used in the medium of print is not limited to engineering schools, but is rife in our entire educational system. The time has come to remove this bias and treat the various media as equal, so that our educational system will reflect the messages of those media with which children and adults spend a large part of their lives.

References
Suggested Reading
Index

References

1. THE ELECTRONIC MEDIA

1. B. A. Krier, "Practitioners of the Art of Zen TV Watching," *Los Angeles Times,* June 6, 1982, pt. VIII, pp. 1, 14.
2. H. T. Himmelweit, A. N. Oppenheim, and P. Vince, *Television and the Child: An Empirical Study of the Effect of Television on the Young* (London: Oxford University Press, 1958). W. Schramm, J. Lyle, and E. B. Parker, *Television in the Lives of Our Children* (Stanford, Calif.: Stanford University Press, 1961).
3. M. Winn, *The Plug-In Drug* (New York: Viking, 1977). J. Mander, *Four Arguments for the Elimination of Television* (New York: Quill, 1978).
4. M. McLuhan, *Understanding Media: The Extensions of Man* (New York: McGraw-Hill, 1964).
5. J. S. Bruner, personal communication, 1982.
6. McLuhan, *Understanding Media,* p. 30.
7. Himmelweit, Oppenheim, and Vince, *Television and the Child.*
8. S. Gadberry and M. Schneider, "Effects of Parental Restrictions on TV-Viewing," paper presented to the American Psychological Association, 1978.
9. National Institute of Mental Health, *Television and Behavior: Ten Years of Scientific Progress and Implications for the Eighties,* vol. 1, *Summary Report* (Rockville, Md.: 1982).

2. FILM AND TELEVISION LITERACY

1. M. L. Rice, A. C. Huston, and J. C. Wright, "The Forms of Television: Effects on Children's Attention, Comprehension, and Social Behavior," in D. Pearl, L. Bouthilet, and J. Lazar, eds., *Television and Behavior: Ten Years of Scientific Progress and Implications for the Eighties,* vol. 2, *Technical Reviews* (Rockville, Md.: National Institute of Mental Health, 1982). J. D. Andrew, "Christian Metz and the Semiology of the Cinema," in Andrew, *The Major Film*

Theories (Oxford: Oxford University Press, 1976). G. Salomon, *Interaction of Media, Cognition, and Learning* (San Francisco: Jossey-Bass, 1979).

2. Andrew, "Christian Metz."

3. W. A. Collins, "Cognitive Processing in Television Viewing," in Pearl, Bouthilet, and Lazar, eds., *Television and Behavior*.

4. R. Smith, "Preschool Children's Comprehension of Television," paper presented at the Biennial Meeting of the Society for Research in Child Development, April 1981. D. R. Anderson and R. Smith, "Young Children's TV Viewing: The Problem of Cognitive Continuity," in F. J. Morrison, C. Lord, and D. F. Keating, eds., *Advances in Applied Developmental Psychology* (New York: Academic Press, in press).

5. W. A. Collins, "Children's Comprehension of Television Content," in E. Wartella, ed., *Children Communicating: Media and Development of Thought, Speech, Understanding* (Beverly Hill, Calif.: Sage, 1979).

6. R. Smith, D. R. Anderson, and C. Fischer, "Young Children's Comprehension of Cinematic Techniques," paper presented at the Biennial Meeting of the Society for Research in Child Development, April 1983. Anderson and Smith, "Young Children's TV Viewing."

7. G. Noble, *Children in Front of the Small Screen* (London: Constable, 1975).

8. G. Salomon and A. A. Cohen, "Television Formats, Mastery of Mental Skills, and the Acquisition of Knowledge," *Journal of Educational Psychology,* 1977, *69,* 612–619.

9. Salomon, *Interaction of Media, Cognition, and Learning.*

10. R. E. Snow, J. Tiffin, and W. F. Seibert, "Individual Differences and Instructional Film Effects," *Journal of Educational Psychology,* 1965, *56,* 315–326.

11. Salomon, *Interaction of Media, Cognition, and Learning.*

12. Rice, Huston, and Wright, "The Forms of Television." B. A. Watkins, A. Huston-Stein, and J. C. Wright, "Effects of Planned Television Programming," in E. L. Palmer and A. Dorr, eds., *Children and the Faces of Television: Teaching, Violence, Selling* (New York: Academic Press, 1980).

13. E. L. Palmer, "A Pedagogical Analysis of Recurrent Formats on *Sesame Street* and *The Electric Company*," paper presented at the International Conference on Children's Educational Television, Amsterdam, June 1978, and the Annual Convention of the National Association of Educational Broadcasters, Washington, D.C., October 1978.
14. Ibid.
15. *Newsweek*, May 26, 1982. *Time*, May 31, 1982, p. 59.

3. TELEVISION AND LEARNING

1. E. L. Palmer, "Formative Research in Educational Television Production: The Experience of the Children's Television Workshop," in W. Schramm, ed., *Quality in Instructional Television* (Honolulu: University Press of Hawaii, 1972). A. C. Huston and J. C. Wright, "Children's Processing of Television: The Informative Functions of Formal Features," in J. Bryant and D. R. Anderson, eds., *Watching TV, Understanding TV: Research on Children's Attention and Comprehension* (New York: Academic Press, 1983). I. Rydin, "Children's Understanding of Television. II. From Seed to Telephone Pole, With Moving Picture or Stills?" Swedish Broadcasting Corporation, 1979.
2. L. Meringoff, "A Story, A Story: The Influence of the Medium on Children's Apprehension of Stories," *Journal of Educational Psychology*, 1980, 72, 240–249.
3. C. M. Murphy and D. J. Wood, "Learning through Media: A Comparison of 4-8-Year-Old Children's Responses to Filmed and Pictorial Instruction," unpublished paper, University of Nottingham, 1981.
4. Rydin, "Children's Understanding of Television."
5. G. C. Sparks and J. Cantor, "Developmental Differences in Responses to *The Incredible Hulk*: Using Piaget's Theory of Cognitive Development to Predict Emotional Effects," unpublished paper, University of Wisconsin, Madison, n.d.
6. H. Sturm and S. Jorg, *Information Processing by Young Children: Piaget's Theory Applied to Radio and Television* (Munich: K. G. Saur, 1981).

186 / References

7. G. S. Lesser, *Children and Television: Lessons from Sesame Street* (New York: Random House, 1974).
8. N. Sproull, "Visual Attention, Modeling Behaviors, and Other Verbal and Nonverbal Meta-Communication of Prekindergarten Children Viewing *Sesame Street*," *American Educational Research Journal*, 1973, *10*, 101–114.
9. G. Dunn, *The Box in the Corner: Television and the Under-Fives* (London: Macmillan, 1977).
10. Ibid.
11. A. Hobsbaum and C. Ghikas, "*You and Me*: An Investigation into the Short Term Effectiveness of the BBC Television Series," BBC School Broadcasts, Research and Evaluation Report, no. 5, Autumn 1979.
12. IBA Audience Research Department, *Children and Television: A Survey of the Role of TV in Children's Experience, and of Parents' Attitudes towards TV for Their Children* (London: Independent Broadcasting Authority, 1974). J. L. Singer and D. G. Singer, *Television, Imagination, and Aggression: A Study of Preschoolers* (Hillsdale, N.J.: Erlbaum, 1981).

4. TELEVISION AND SOCIAL REALITY

1. A. Dorr, "Television and the Socialization of the Minority Child," in G. L. Berry and C. Mitchell-Kernan, eds., *Television and the Socialization of the Minority Child* (New York: Academic Press, 1982). R. P. Hawkins and S. Pingree, "Television's Influence on Social Reality," in Pearl, Bouthilet, and Lazar, eds., *Television and Behavior*. A. Dorr Leifer, "Research on the Socialization Influence of Television in the United States," *Fernsehen und Bildung*, 1975, *9*, 111–142. Noble, *Children in Front of the Small Screen*.
2. B. S. Greenberg, "Television and Role Socialization: An Overview," in Pearl, Bouthilet, and Lazar, eds., *Television and Behavior*.
3. H. F. Waters, "Life According to TV," *Newsweek*, December 6, 1982, p. 136.
4. M. Lalor, "The Hidden Curriculum," in R. Rogers, ed., *Television and the Family* (London: UK Association for the

International Year of the Child and the University of London, 1980).

5. A. S. Tan, "TV Beauty Ads and Role Expectations of Adolescent Female Viewers," *Journalism Quarterly*, 1979, 56, 283–288.

6. Himmelweit, Oppenheim, and Vince, *Television and the Child.* C. V. Feilitzen, L. Filipson, and I. Schyller, *Open Your Eyes to Children's Viewing: On Children, TV and Radio, Now and in the Future* (Stockholm: Sveriges Radios forlag, 1977).

7. R. P. Ross, T. Campbell, J. C. Wright, A. C. Huston, M. L. Rice, and P. Turk, "When Celebrities Talk, Children Listen: An Experimental Analysis of Children's Responses to TV Ads with Celebrity Endorsement," unpublished paper, Center for Research on the Influences of Television on Children, University of Kansas, n.d.

8. J. Johnston and J. Ettema, *Positive Images: Breaking Stereotypes with Children's Television* (Beverly Hills, Calif.: Sage, 1982).

9. C. R. Corder-Bolz, "Mediation: The Role of Significant Others," *Journal of Communication*, 1980, 30, 106–118.

10. K. Durkin, *Sex Roles and Children's Television*, Report to the Independent Broadcasting Authority, Social Psychology Research Unit, University of Kent, Canterbury, 1983.

11. H. Fairchild, "Creating, Producing, and Evaluating Prosocial TV: Reflections of a Social Scientist," unpublished paper, UCLA, n.d.

12. Greenberg, "Television and Role Socialization."

13. G. Bogatz and S. Ball, *The Second Year of "Sesame Street": A Continuing Evaluation* (Princeton, N.J.: Educational Testing Service, 1971). P. G. Christenson and D. F. Roberts, "The Role of Television in the Formation of Children's Social Attitudes," in M. J. A. Howe, ed., *Learning from Television: Psychological and Educational Research* (London: Academic Press, 1982).

14. Dorr, "Television and the Socialization of the Minority Child."

15. S. B. Graves, "Television and Its Impact on the Cognitive and Affective Development of Minority Children," in Berry

and Mitchell-Kernan, eds., *Television and the Socialization of the Minority Child.*

16. Feilitzen, Filipson, and Schyller, *Open Your Eyes to Children's Viewing,* pp. 50–51. S. Guskin, W. Morgan, M. Cherkes, and T. Peel, "The Effects of *Sesame Street* Segments about Deafness and Signing on Four and Five Year Olds' Understandings and Attitudes," Children's Television Workshop, 1979.

17. C. L. O'Brien, "The *Big Blue Marble* Story," *Television and Children,* 1981, 4/5, 18–22. Christenson and Roberts, "The Role of Television in the Formation of Children's Social Attitudes."

18. Himmelweit, Oppenheim, and Vince, *Television and the Child.*

19. R. C. Peterson and L. L. Thurstone, *Motion Pictures and the Social Attitudes of Children* (New York: Macmillan, 1933). Christenson and Roberts, "The Role of Television in the Formation of Children's Social Attitudes."

20. Feilitzen, Filipson, and Schyller, *Open Your Eyes to Children's Viewing,* p. 51.

21. Himmelweit, Oppenheim, and Vince, *Television and the Child.*

22. Noble, *Children in Front of the Small Screen,* p. 62.

23. *Media Watch Bulletin* (Chapel Hill, N.C.), 1981. D. G. Singer, "The Research Connection," *Television and Children,* 1982, 5, 25–35.

24. L. R. Huesmann, "Television Violence and Aggressive Behavior," in Pearl, Bouthilet, and Lazar, eds., *Television and Behavior.* J. P. Rushton, "Television and Prosocial Behavior," in Pearl, Bouthilet, and Lazar, eds., *Television and Behavior.*

25. Rushton, "Television and Prosocial Behavior."

26. A. Dorr, "Television and Affective Development and Functioning," in Pearl, Bouthilet, and Lazar, eds., *Television and Behavior.*

27. H. Sturm, "Emotional Effects—Media-Specific Factors in Radio and Television: Results of Two Studies and Projected Research," *Fernsehen und Bildung,* 1978, 12.

28. R. S. Drabman and M. H. Thomas, "Does Media Violence

Increase Children's Toleration of Real-Life Aggression?"
Developmental Psychology, 1974, *10*, 418–424. H. F. Waters,
"What TV Does to Kids," *Newsweek*, February 21, 1977,
pp. 62–70.

29. Himmelweit, Oppenheim, and Vince, *Television and the Child*.

30. Ibid.

31. G. Comstock, S. Chaffee, N. Katzman, M. McCombs, and D. Roberts, *Television and Human Behavior* (New York: Columbia University Press, 1978). J. P. Murray and S. Kippax, "From the Early Window to the Late Night Show: International Trends in the Study of Television's Impact on Children and Adults," in L. Berkowitz, ed., *Advances in Experimental Social Psychology* (New York: Academic Press, 1979).

32. S. Feshbach, N. Feshbach, and S. E. Cohen, "Enhancing Children's Discrimination in Response to Television Advertising: The Effects of Psychoeducational Training in Two Elementary-School-Age Groups," *Developmental Review*, in press.

33. A. Dorr, "When I Was a Child, I Thought as a Child," in S. B. Withey and R. P. Abeles, eds., *Television and Social Behavior: Beyond Violence and Children* (Hillsdale, N.J.: Erlbaum, 1980), p. 195.

34. A. Dorr, "No Short Cuts to Judging Reality," in Bryant and Anderson, eds., *Watching TV, Understanding TV*. Dorr, "When I Was a Child I Thought as a Child." D. E. Fernie, "Ordinary and Extraordinary People," in H. Kelly and H. Gardner, eds., *Viewing Children through Television* (San Francisco: Jossey-Bass, 1981).

35. Noble, *Children in Front of the Small Screen*. Fernie, "Ordinary and Extraordinary People."

36. H. Kelly, "Reasoning about Realities: Children's Evaluations of Television and Books," in Kelly and Gardner, eds., *Viewing Children through Television*.

37. Feilitzen, Filipson, and Schyller, *Open Your Eyes to Children's Viewing*.

38. Dorr, "Television and the Socialization of the Minority Child."

39. A. F. Newcomb, and W. A. Collins, "Children's Comprehension of Family Role Portrayals in Televised Dramas: Effects of Socio-Economic Status, Ethnicity, and Age," *Developmental Psychology*, 1979, *15*, 417–423.

40. L. S. Liben and M. L. Signorella, "Gender-Related Schemata and Constructive Memory in Children," *Child Development*, 1980, *5*, 11–18.

41. S. Pingree, "The Effects of Nonsexist Television Commercials and Perceptions of Reality on Children's Attitudes about Women,"*Psychology of Women Quarterly*, 1978, *2*, 262–276. Durkin, *Sex Roles and Children's Television*.

42. C. R. Corder-Bolz, "Television Literacy and Critical Viewing Skills," in Pearl, Bouthilet, and Lazar, eds., *Television and Behavior*.

43. C. R. Corder-Bolz and S. L. O'Bryant, "Can People Affect Television? Teacher vs. Program," *Journal of Communication*, 1978, *28*, 97–103.

44. J. Bryce, "Family Styles and Television Use," paper presented to the Conference on Culture and Communication, Philadelphia, April 1981. D. G. Singer and J. L. Singer, "Family Lifestyle and Television-Viewing as Predictors of Children's Cognition, Imagination and Motor Behavior," paper presented to the Society for Research in Child Development, Detroit, April 1983.

45. Himmelweit, Oppenheim, and Vince, *Television and the Child*. A. A. Cohen, H. Adoni, and G. Drori, "Adolescents' Differential Perception of Social Conflicts in Television News and Social Reality" unpublished paper, Hebrew University of Jerusalem, 1982.

46. A. Dorr, S. B. Graves, and E. Phelps, "Television Literacy for Young Children," *Journal of Communication*, 1980, *30*, 71–83.

5. USING TELEVISION TO OVERCOME EDUCATIONAL
   DISADVANTAGE

1. H. Himmelweit, personal communication, 1983.
2. T. D. Cook, H. Appleton, R. F. Conner, A. Shaffer,

G. Tamkin, and S. J. Weber, *Sesame Street Revisited* (New York: Russell Sage, 1975). G. Salomon, *"Sesame Street in Israel: Its Instructional and Psychological Effects on Children,"* unpublished paper, Hebrew University of Jerusalem, 1974. S. Ball and G. A. Bogatz, *The First Year of "Sesame Street": An Evaluation* (Princeton, N.J.: Educational Testing Service, 1970). K. I. Lemercier and G. R. Teasdale, " 'Sesame Street': Some Effects of a Television Programme on the Cognitive Skills of Young Children from Lower SES Backgrounds," *Australian Psychologist*, 1973, *8*, 47–51. Lesser, *Children and Television.*

3. Lesser, *Children and Television.*
4. S. Y. Gibbon, Jr., E. L. Palmer, and B. R. Fowles, *"Sesame Street, The Electric Company*, and Reading," in J. B. Carroll and J. S. Chall, eds., *Toward a Literate Society* (New York: McGraw-Hill, 1975).
5. J. G. Cooney, *"The Electric Company*—Television and Reading, 1971–1980: A Mid-Experiment Appraisal," Children's Television Workshop, 1976. S. Ball, G. A. Bogatz, K. M. Kazarow, and D. B. Rubin, *Reading with Television: A Follow-Up Evaluation of The Electric Company* (Princeton, N.J.: Educational Testing Service, 1974). S. Ball and G. Bogatz, *Reading with the Electric Company* (Princeton, N.J.: Educational Testing Service, 1973).
6. Ball, Bogatz, Kazarow, and Rubin, *Reading with Television.*
7. Gibbon, Palmer, and Fowles, *"Sesame Street, The Electric Company*, and Reading."
8. Huston and Wright, "Children's Processing of Television."
9. Graves, "Television and Its Impact on the Cognitive and Affective Development of Minority Children." Corder-Bolz, "Mediation."
10. Ball and Bogatz, *The First Year of "Sesame Street."* Salomon, *"Sesame Street* in Israel."
11. My description of Téléniger and its results comes from the following sources: W. Schramm, *Big Media, Little Media* (Beverly Hills, Calif.: Sage, 1977). M. Egly, "Téléniger," *Dossiers Pedagogiques*, 1973, *1*, 2–5. E. Pierre, "La Com-

munication Classe-Ecran: Un Relation d'Apprentissage," *Dossiers Pedagogiques*, 1973, *1*, 6–11.

12. R. Diaz-Guerrero, I. Reyes-Lagunes, D. B. Witzke, and W. H. Holtzman, "*Plaza Sesamo* in Mexico: An Evaluation," *Journal of Communication*, 1976, *26*, 109–123.

13. H. Himmelweit, "Youth, Television, and Experimentation," in *Cultural Role of Broadcasting* (Tokyo: Hoso-Bunka Foundation, 1978).

14. J. K. Mayo, R. C. Hornik, and E. G. McAnany, *Educational Reform with Television: The El Salvador Experience* (Stanford: Stanford University Press, 1976).

6. COMPARING PRINT, RADIO, AND TELEVISION

1. S. Scribner and M. Cole, *The Psychology of Literacy* (Cambridge, Mass.: Harvard University Press, 1981).

2. M. Wober, "Individualism, Home Life, and Work Efficiency among a Group of Nigerian Workers," *Journal of Occupational Psychology*, 1967, *41*, 183–192.

3. McLuhan, *Understanding Media*, p. 31.

4. J. P. Murray, *Television and Youth: Twenty-Five Years of Research and Controversy* (Boys Town, Neb.: Boys Town Center for the Study of Youth Development, 1980).

5. K. Pezdek and A. Lehrer, "The Relationship between Reading and Cognitive Processing of Media," unpublished paper, Claremont Graduate School, 1983.

6. G. Salomon, "Toward a Theory of Communication and Education in Reciprocal Relations: Learners' Active Role," address to the American Psychological Association, Anaheim, Calif., August 1983.

7. M. Morgan and L. Gross, "Television and Educational Achievement and Aspiration," in Pearl, Bouthilet, and Lazar, eds., *Television and Behavior*.

8. G. Salomon, "Television Watching and Mental Effort: A Social Psychological View," in Bryant and Anderson, eds., *Watching TV, Understanding TV*.

9. C. A. Char and L. Meringoff, "The Role of Story Illustrations: Children's Story Comprehension in Three Dif-

ferent Media," Harvard Project Zero, Technical Report no. 22, January 1981.

10. P. Greenfield, "Radio and Television Experimentally Compared: Effects of the Medium on Imagination and Transmission of Content," final report to National Institute of Education, Teaching and Learning Program, 1982. J. Beagles-Roos and I. Gat, "Specific Impact of Radio and Television on Children's Story Comprehension," *Journal of Educational Psychology*, 1983, *75*, 128–137.

11. L. Meringoff, "The Influence of the Medium on Children's Story Apprehension, *Journal of Educational Psychology*, 1980, *72*, 240–249. L. K. Meringoff, M. M. Vibbert, C. A. Char, D. E. Fernie, G. S. Banker, and H. Gardner, "How is Children's Learning from Television Distinctive?: Exploiting the Medium Methodologically," in Bryant and Anderson, eds., *Watching TV, Understanding TV*.

12. D. Hayes and D. W. Birnbaum, "Preschoolers' Retention of Televised Events: Is a Picture Worth a Thousand Words?" *Developmental Psychology*, 1980, *16*, 410–416.

13. Pezdek and Lehrer, "The Relationship between Reading and Cognitive Processing of Media." K. Pezdek and E. Stevens, "Children's Memory for Auditory and Visual Information on Television," *Developmental Psychology*, forthcoming.

14. Char and Meringoff, in a study similar to ours, did not find an advantage in dialogue recall for radio. However, they had children of equivalent age to our younger ones, and we found these children recalled relatively little dialogue no matter what the medium. In addition, Char and Meringoff used a much smaller sample than we did. These two factors seem sufficient to account for the discrepancy between their results and ours.

15. D. Jennings, "Children's Comprehension of Television Programmes," B.Sc. project, London School of Economics, 1982.

16. P. G. Zukow, J. Reilly, and P. M. Greenfield, "Making the Absent Present: Facilitating the Transition from Sensori-Motor to Linguistic Communication," in K. Nelson, ed., *Children's Language*, vol. 3 (New York: Gardner Press, 1982).

17. A. R. Hollenbeck and R. G. Slaby, "Infant Visual and Vocal Responses to Television," *Child Development*, 1979, *50*, 41–45.

18. Pezdek and Stevens, "Children's Memory for Auditory and Visual Information on Television."

19. P. Baggett, "Structurally Equivalent Stories in Movie and Text and the Effect of the Medium on Recall," *Journal of Verbal Learning and Verbal Behavior*, 1979, *18*, 333–356.

20. P. Greenfield, B. Geber, J. Beagles-Roos, D. Farrar, and I. Gat, "Television and Radio Experimentally Compared: Effects of the Medium on Imagination and Transmission of Content," paper presented at the Biennial Meeting of the Society for Research in Child Development, Boston, April 1981.

21. J. L. Singer and D. G. Singer, *Television, Imagination, and Aggression*. Singer and Singer, "Family Lifestyle and Television-Viewing." L. F. Harrison and T. M. Williams, "Television and Cognitive Development," in The Impact of Television: A Natural Experiment Involving Three Communities, a symposium presented to the Canadian Psychological Association, Vancouver, 1977.

22. J. L. Singer and D. G. Singer, "Can TV Stimulate Imaginative Play?" *Journal of Communication*, 1976, *26*, 74–80. R. B. Tower, D. G. Singer, and J. L. Singer, "Differential Effects of Television Programming on Preschoolers' Cognition, Imagination, and Social Play," *American Journal of Orthopsychiatry*, 1979, *49*, 265–281. M. A. Runco and K. Pezdek, "The Effect of Television and Radio on Children's Creativity," unpublished paper, Claremont Graduate School, 1982. Himmelweit, Oppenheim, and Vince, *Television and the Child*.

23. L. K. Meringoff, M. Vibbert, H. Kelly, and C. Char, "How Shall You Take Your Story with or without Pictures?: Progress Report on a Program of Media Research with Children," paper presented at the Biennial Meeting of the Society for Research in Child Development, April 1981.

24. Feilitzen, Filipson, and Schyller, *Open Your Eyes to Children's Viewing*.

25. Greenfield, "Radio and Television Experimentally Com-

pared." Beagles-Roos and Gat, "Specific Impact of Radio and Television." C. W. Meline, "Does the Medium Matter?" *Journal of Communication*, 1976, *26*, 81–89.
26. Himmelweit, Oppenheim, and Vince, *Television and the Child*.
27. Gadberry and Schneider, "Effects of Parental Restrictions on TV-Viewing."
28. Singer and Singer, "Family Lifestyle and Television-Viewing."
29. T. M. Williams, personal communication, 1983.
30. D. R. Anderson, S. R. Levin, and E. P. Lorch, "The Effects of TV Program Pacing on the Behavior of Preschool Children," *AV Communication Review*, 1977, *25*, 159–166.

7. VIDEO GAMES

1. B. D. Brooks, presentation at conference on Video Games and Human Development, A Research Agenda for the '80s, Harvard Graduate School of Education, May 1983.
2. E. Mitchell, presentation at conference on Video Games and Human Development, A Research Agenda for the '80s, Harvard Graduate School of Education, May 1983.
3. D. R. Anderson, "Home Television Viewing by Preschool Children and their Families," paper presented to the Society for Research in Child Development, April 1983.
4. H. Gardner, "When Television Marries Computers," review of *Pilgrim in the Microworld* by Robert Sudnow, *New York Times*, March 27, 1983, p. 12.
5. T. W. Malone, "What Makes Things Fun to Learn? A Study of Intrinsically Motivating Computer Games." Cognitive and Instructional Science Series, CIS-7 (SSL-80-11), Xerox Palo Alto Research Center, Palo Alto, Calif. T. W. Malone, "Toward a Theory of Intrinsically Motivating Instruction," *Cognitive Science*, 1981, *5*, 333–370.
6. S. B. Rosenfeld. "Informal Learning and Computers," position paper prepared for the Atari Institute for Education-Action Research, June 1982.
7. D. Anderson, *Informal Features*, 1982, p. 9.
8. S. B. Silvern, P. A. Williamson, and T. A. Countermine,

"Video Game Playing and Aggression in Young Children," paper presented to the American Educational Research Association, 1983.

9. S. B. Silvern, P. A. Williamson, and T. A. Countermine, "Video Game Play and Social Behavior: Preliminary Findings," paper presented at the International Conference on Play and Play Environments, 1983.

10. Huston and Wright, "Children's Processing of Television."

11. B. A. Lauber, "Adolescent Video Game Use," unpublished paper, UCLA, 1983.

12. In this description of the game I draw on J. Sykora and J. Birkner, *The Video Master's Guide to Pac-Man* (New York: Bantam, 1982).

13. Singer and Singer, *Television, Imagination, and Aggression*.

14. T. M. Kahn, "An Analysis of Strategic Thinking Using a Computer-Based Game," Ph.D. diss., University of California, Berkeley, 1981.

15. E. Wanner, "Computer Time: The Electronic Boogeyman," *Psychology Today*, October 1982, *16*, 8–11.

16. "School Uses of Microcomputers: Reports from a National Survey," Center for Social Organization of Schools, Johns Hopkins University, April 1983.

17. Laboratory of Comparative Human Cognition, "A Model System for the Study of Learning Difficulties," *Quarterly Newsletter of the Laboratory of Comparative Human Cognition*, 1982, *4*, 39–66, p. 57.

18. J. D. Chaffin, B. Maxwell, and B. Thompson, "ARC-ED Curriculum: The Application of Video Game Formats to Educational Software," *Exceptional Children*, 1982, *49*, 173–178. M. C. Linn, "Assessing the Cognitive Consequences of Computer Learning: Research Findings and Policy Implications," symposium at the American Educational Research Association, 1983. S. Chipman, personal communication, 1983.

19. J. A. Levin and Y. Kareev, "Personal Computers and Education: The Challenge to Schools," CHIP 98, Center for Human Information Processing, University of California, San Diego, 1980, pp. 40–41.

8. COMPUTERS

1. "School Uses of Microcomputers."
2. *Los Angeles Times,* June 28, 1983.
3. *Don't Bother Me, I'm Learning: Adventures in Computer Education* (Del Mar, Calif.: CRM/McGraw-Hill, 1982).
4. J. A. Levin, "Computers in Non-School Settings: Implications for Education," *SIGCUE Bulletin,* June 1982.
5. D. Brown, "Computer Teaching in the Year 1982," presentation at a colloquium, Conscious and Unconscious Mental Processes: Implications for Learning, University of California, Berkeley, June 1982.
6. H. Kohl, "Should I Buy My Child a Computer?" *Harvard Magazine,* September-October 1982, 14–21.
7. D. M. Kurland, "Software for the Classroom: Issues in the Design of Effective Software Tools," in *Chameleon in the Classroom: Developing Roles for Computers,* Technical Report no. 22, Bank Street College of Education, New York, 1983.
8. J. F. Vinsonhaler and R. K. Bass, "A Summary of Ten Major Studies of CAI Drill and Practice," *Educational Technology,* 1972, *12,* 29–32.
9. M. Ragosta, P. W. Holland, and D. T. Jameson, "Computer Assisted Instruction and Compensatory Education: The ETS/LAUSD Study," final report to the National Institute of Education, 1982.
10. L. H. Sandals, "Computer-Assisted Applications for Learning with Special Needs Children," ERIC no. ED173983, 1979. J. J. Winters et al.,"The Instructional Use of CAI in the Education of the Mentally Retarded," ERIC no. ED157333, 1978.
11. F. Golden, "Here Come the Microkids," *Time,* May 3, 1982, p. 44. M. V. Covington and R. G. Beery, *Self-Worth and School Learning* (New York: Holt, Rinehart, and Winston, 1976).
12. J. A. Levin, "Estimation Techniques for Arithmetic: Everyday Math and Mathematics Instruction," *Educational Studies in Mathematics,* 1981, *12,* 421–434, p. 426.
13. J. A. Levin and Y. Kareev, "Problem Solving in Everyday

Situations," *Quarterly Newsletter of the Laboratory of Comparative Human Cognition*, 1980, *2*, 47–52, p. 49.

14. J. H. Kane, "Computers for Composing," in *Chameleon in the Classroom*. K. Sheingold, personal communication, 1983.
15. Atari, *A Guide to Computers in Education* (Sunnyvale, Calif., 1982), p. 13.
16. G. N. Ebersole, "Microcomputers in the Classroom: Electronic Carrots," *Today's Education*, 1982, *71*, 24–26.
17. W. R. Hughes, "A Study of the Use of Computer Simulated Experiments in the Physics Classroom," *Journal of Computer Based Instruction*, 1974, *1*, 1–6.
18. S. Papert, *Mindstorms* (New York: Basic Books, 1980).
19. Kane, "Computers for Composing."
20. Ibid.
21. J. Hawkins, personal communication, 1982.
22. J. McGee, "Paradise Gained: A Computer for the English Teacher," presentation to the National Education Association, July 1982.
23. B. A. Krier, "A Word-Processing Romance," *Los Angeles Times*, July 7, 1982, pt. V, p. 4.
24. J. A. Levin, M. J. Boruta, and M. T. Vasconcellos, "Microcomputer-Based Environments for Writing," in A. C. Wilkinson, ed., *Classroom Computers and Cognitive Science* (New York: Academic Press, in press).
25. Ibid.
26. Papert, *Mindstorms*, p. 30.
27. S. Scribner, "The Cognitive Consequences of Literacy," unpublished paper, City University of New York, 1969.
28. Kane, "Computers for Composing."
29. L. M. Gomez, C. Bowers, and D. E. Egan, "Learner Characteristics that Predict Success in Using a Text-Editor Tutorial," *Proceedings of Human Factors in Computer Systems*, Gaithersburg, Md., March 1982. L. M. Gomez, D. E. Egan, E. A. Wheeler, D. K. Sharma, and A. M. Gruchacz, "How Interface Design Determines Who Has Difficulty Learning to Use a Text Editor." In *Proceedings of the Human Factors in Computing Systems Conference*, Boston, December 1983.
30. National Institute of Education (S. Chipman), "The Cog-

nitive Demands and Consequences of Computer Learning," Request for Proposal NIE-R-62-0011, 1982, p. 2.
31. M. Harris, "Here Come the Microteens," *Money*, March 1982, 67–68.
32. R. D. Pea and D. M. Kurland, "On the Cognitive and Educational Benefits of Teaching Children Programming: A Critical Look," *New Ideas in Psychology*, 1983, 1, forthcoming.
33. Papert, *Mindstorms*, p. 30.
34. Pea and Kurland, "On the Cognitive and Educational Benefits of Teaching Children Programming."
35. Ibid.
36. A. DiSessa, "LOGO Project, Massachusetts Institute of Technology," in T. W. Malone and J. Levin, eds., *Microcomputers in Education: Cognitive and Social Design Principles*, Report of a Conference, University of California, San Diego, March 1981.
37. A. DiSessa, "Unlearning Aristotelian Physics," *Cognitive Science*, 1982, 6, 37–75.
38. Pea and Kurland, "On the Cognitive and Educational Benefits of Teaching Children Programming."
39. J. Hawkins, K. Sheingold, M. Gearhart, and C. Berger, "Microcomputers in Schools: Impact on the Social Life of Elementary Classrooms," *Applied Developmental Psychology*, 1982, 3, 361–373.
40. O. K. Tikhomirov, "Man and Computer: The Impact of Computer Technology on the Development of Psychological Processes," in D. E. Olson, ed., *Media and Symbols: The Forms of Expression, Communication, and Education* (Chicago: National Society for the Study of Education and University of Chicago Press, 1974).
41. R. Montemayor, "Eastside Students Plug In to the Computer Age," *Los Angeles Times*, August 28, 1983, p. 1.

9. MULTIMEDIA EDUCATION

1. J. Johnston and J. S. Ettema, *Positive Images* (Beverly Hills: Sage, 1982).

2. D. Singer, Conference on Children and Television, Boystown, Nebraska, March 1982.
3. Salomon, "Television Watching and Mental Effort."
4. R. M. Lehman, *Centering Television* (Madison, Wis.: Children/Television/Learning, 1980).
5. E. Levinson, *Effects of Motion Pictures on the Response to Narrative*, ERIC no. ED003567, 1962. This is not a perfectly controlled study, because the students who merely read the story were exposed to it only once while the students who both read the story and saw the film were exposed to it twice. But from the point of view of ecological validity this does not seem to be a significant criticism, because, in the real world of school, students do not read literature twice, nor would it be practical to expect them to do so.
6. R. L. Potter, "Television and Teaching: The Emerging Partnership," *Television and Children*, 1982, 5, 24–25. Himmelweit, Oppenheim, and Vince, *Television and the Child*.
7. R. L. Potter, "TV and My Classroom: An Evolutionary Tale," *Television and Children*, 1979, 2, 19–20.
8. "Television for Learning: A Catalog of Reading Programs and Teachers' Guides," *Television and Children*, 1979, 2, 36–38. A. Dorr Leifer, "Teaching with Television and Film," in N. L. Gage, ed., *Psychology of Teaching Methods*, National Society for the Study of Education Yearbook (Chicago: University of Chicago Press, 1976).
9. Collins, "Children's Comprehension of Television Content."
10. S. Neuwirth, "Using Television to Teach Story Comprehension: One Teacher's Experience," *Television and Children*, 1982, 5, 36–38, p. 37.
11. M. L. Scarborough, "The Educational Value of Non-Educational Television: A Study of Children's Response to General Programme Material," Independent Broadcasting Authority, London, 1973.
12. Schramm, *Big Media, Little Media*.
13. J. S. Bruner, personal communication, 1982.
14. R. Lundgren, "What Is a Good Instructional Program," in Schramm, ed., *Quality in Instructional Television*, pp. 13–14.

15. S. Chipman, "French Activities Related to Computers and Education," National Institute of Education, n.d.
16. Kurland, "Software for the Classroom."
17. Levin and Kareev, "Personal Computers and Education."
18. Dorr Leifer, "Teaching with Television and Film." K. W. Mielke, "Barriers to Classroom Use of *The Electric Company*," Children's Television Workshop, 1977.
19. M. Wober, personal communication, 1983.
20. D. R. Olson, *Cognitive Development: The Child's Acquisition of Diagonality* (New York: Academic Press, 1970).
21. G. Salomon, "Television Literacy and Television vs. Literacy," in R. W. Bailey and R. M. Fostein, eds., *Literacy for Life: The Demand for Reading and Writing* (New York: Modern Language Association, 1983).
22. E. S. Ferguson, "The Mind's Eye: Nonverbal Thought in Technology," *Science*, 1977, *197*, 827–836.

Suggested Reading

PRACTICAL BOOKS FOR PARENTS

E. Keye, *The Family Guide to Children's Television* (New York: Random House, 1974). Like the other books for parents listed here, this one focuses on television in the United States.

K. Moody, *Growing Up on Television* (New York: Times Books, 1980). A good digest of television's negative effects.

D. G. Singer, J. L. Singer, and D. M. Zuckerman, *Teaching Television: How to Use TV to Your Child's Advantage* (New York: Dial Press, 1981). This book presents a curriculum on critical viewing skills for parents to use with young children, as well as an excellent list of sources for television-related materials. This list would be equally valuable for teachers.

FOR TEACHERS

B. Logan, ed., *Television Awareness Training* (New York: Media Action Research Center, 1977). This book, with the addition of film information and other resources available from Media Action Research Center, could be the basis for a junior high school or high school course in critical viewing skills. The book includes reading materials for students and teachers from a wide variety of sources, as well as worksheets and homework assignments.

L. Masterman, *Teaching about Television* (London: Macmillan, 1980). Using examples from British television, Masterman presents the rationale and lesson plans for a secondary school course in television studies. These lessons treat television primarily as literature, as culture, and as nonverbal communication.

RESEARCH AND THEORY

G. Berry and C. Mitchell-Kernan, eds., *Television and the Socialization of the Minority Child* (New York: Academic

Press, 1982). The authoritative book in this important area.

J. Bryant and D. R. Anderson, eds., *Watching TV, Understanding TV: Research on Children's Attention and Comprehension* (New York: Academic Press, 1983). The state of the art in cognitive research on the relationship between children and television.

H. T. Himmelweit, A. N. Oppenheim, and P. Vince, *Television and the Child: An Empirical Study of the Effect of Television on the Young* (London: Oxford University Press, 1958). The classic empirical study of children and television. Using the interview method, the researchers came up with many findings that are now being duplicated with other techniques.

J. Johnston and J. Ettema, *Positive Images: Breaking Stereotypes with Children's Television* (Beverly Hills, Calif.: Sage, 1982). Particularly valuable for its highly readable account of the development of the series *Freestyle*.

G. S. Lesser, *Children and Television: Lessons from Sesame Street* (New York: Random House, 1974). An account of all aspects of *Sesame Street* from the program's chief academic adviser.

M. McLuhan, *Understanding Media: The Extensions of Man* (New York: McGraw-Hill, 1964). The origin of the idea that "the medium is the message."

G. Noble, *Children in Front of the Small Screen* (London: Constable, 1975). An original and creative treatment of the cognitive and social effects of television on children.

E. L. Palmer and A. Dorr, eds., *Children and the Faces of Television: Teaching, Violence, Selling* (New York: Academic Press, 1980). Contributions from people representing a wide variety of academic disciplines, as well as the media.

S. Papert, *Mindstorms* (New York: Basic Books, 1980). The most influential book about children and computers. Papert's emphasis is on children as programmers, with examples drawn from his experience in teaching LOGO.

D. Pearl, L. Bouthilet, and J. Lazar, eds., *Television and Behavior: Ten Years of Scientific Progress and Implications for the Eighties*, vol. 2, *Technical Reviews* (Rockville, Md.: National Institute of Mental Health, 1982). This follow-up to the 1972 *Report of the Surgeon General's Advisory Committee on Television and Behavior* is an excellent, comprehensive reference source.

S. Scribner and M. Cole, *The Psychology of Literacy* (Cambridge, Mass.: Harvard University Press, 1981). An account of the first empirical research to assess the psychological effects of literacy apart from the effects of formal schooling.

SOFTWARE

All software is for the Apple II unless otherwise noted, although some may be available for other computers.

B. Budge, Pinball Construction Set (Piedmont, Calif.: Budge Co., 1982).

Children's Computer Workshop, Taxi (Fort Worth, Tex.: Radio Shack, 1983).

S. Dugdale, Green Globs, in Graphing Equations (CONDUIT, University of Iowa, Iowa City, 1981).

A. Greenberg and R. Woodhead, Wizardry (Ogdensburg, N.Y.: Sin-Tech Software, 1981).

B. Jamison and C. Kelner, Lemonade Stand (Cupertino, Calif.: Apple Computer, 1979).

L. Klotz, P. Sobalvarro, and S. Hain, supervised by H. Abelson, The Terrapin Logo Language (Cambridge, Mass.: Terrapin, 1981).

W. Robinett, Rocky's Boots (Portola Valley, Calif.: Learning Company, 1982).

S. Warner, Castle Wolfenstein (Baltimore: Muse Software, 1981).

S. Warner, RobotWar (Baltimore: Muse Software, 1981).

R. Wigginton, Animals (Cupertino, Calif.: Apple Computer, 1978).

INDEX